THE BENEFITS OF COLONISATION

ADAM PLOVER

This book is sold subject to the condition that it will not, by way of trade or otherwise, be re-sold, hired out or otherwise circulated without the publisher's prior written consent, in any form of binding or cover other than that in which it is published and without a similar condition, including this condition, being imposed on the subsequent purchaser. No part of this book may be reproduced by any process, stored in a retrieval system, or transmitted in any form without the prior permission of the publisher.

Copyright 2022

ISBN: 9781872970 86 9

Published by:
Tross Publishing,
P. O. Box 22 143,
Khandallah,
Wellington 6441,
New Zealand.

Email: trosspub@gmail.com

BY THE SAME AUTHOR

BLOOD AND TEARS; A Memorial to Those Killed by Tribal and Related Violence.
Price: $30.00

In the course of creating the New Zealand that we have to-day, with its law and order, property rights, personal safety and individual freedom, numerous people - both European and friendly Maori - were killed by tribal violence. They gave their lives in the cause of creating order out of anarchy and are just as deserving of the nation's respect as are soldiers who die on the battle-field.

In this book some of these brave but unfortunate people are introduced to the modern reader, together with brief details of their lives and of their untimely and brutal deaths, thus bringing to life an aspect of our early history that has been overlooked for far too long.

New Zealand's history is being rewritten with a new narrative in favour of the ever growing "grievance industry". In the process real historical events are being swept under the carpet and out of sight if they get in the way of this new agenda. This book, based on facts alone and impeccably researched, tells of some of these long-buried events as they really happened.

For other Tross Publishing books see:
www.trosspublishing.co.nz

TABLE OF CONTENTS

1	A Humanitarian Colonisation	5
2	Food	9
3	Clothing	18
4	Housing	22
5	Transport	26
6	Hygiene	30
7	Health	33
8	Superstition	37
9	Slavery	42
10	Women	48
11	Children	55
12	Infanticide	60
13	Tribal Warfare	64
14	Cannibalism	70
15	Property Rights	79
16	Introduction of Law	86
17	Language	96
18	Fauna and Flora	98
19	Population	103
20	Welcome, White Man	109
	Conclusion	116

CHAPTER 1

A HUMANITARIAN COLONISATION

"In the year 1840 the islands [of New Zealand] became a dependency of the British Crown and the country was beginning to be largely occupied by settlers. This altered state of things brought with it many advantages, and the natives gladly welcomed the change."

Bishop William Williams in *Christianity Among the New Zealanders*[1].

Colonisation by European powers of the world beyond and over the seas had its origin in a Papal Bull, *Inter Caetera*, issued by Pope Alexander VI on 4th May, 1493, which established the "Doctrine of Discovery". This was to support Spain having exclusive rights to the lands that had been discovered by Christopher Columbus the year before. This doctrine became the basis of all European claims in both North and South America and beyond.

Over the ensuing centuries colonisation had a somewhat turbulent history. In South America "Indian groups were entrusted to Spanish proprietors, who in theory cared for them physically and spiritually in return for rights to tribute and labour but who in practice often abused and enslaved them....

The Indians became real or nominal Christians but their numbers shrank, less from slaughter and exploitation than from Old World diseases, frequently smallpox, for which they had no inherited immunity. The aboriginal West Indian population virtually disappeared in a few generations, to be replaced by black slaves. Indian numbers shrank in all mainland areas. At the beginning of Spanish settlement there were perhaps 50,000,000 aborigines; the figure had decreased to an estimated 4,000,000 in the 17th century, after which it slowly rose again".[2]

Fortunately the natives of New Zealand did not suffer in such a way from colonisation even though the Maori is now ethnologically extinct (no full-blooded ones and apparently not even any half-blooded ones). However, this particular "race suicide" was caused not by the colonising power but by the preference of Maoris over the years to breed with Europeans rather than with each other. This choice destroyed their own race and has created a successor race of part-Maoris, with most of those who now claim to be "Maori" having more European blood in them than Maori.

New Zealand was a latecomer in being colonised, the North American colonies dating from 1607, South Africa from 1652 and Australia from 1788. By 1840, when British sovereignty was at last proclaimed over New Zealand after several requests from northern chiefs for this to happen, the Colonial Office in London, the government department that was responsible for colonies, was in the hands of a very powerful group of Evangelical Christians ("humanitarians") who, having recently succeeded in ending slavery throughout the British Empire, were now setting their sights on other worthy causes such as improving the working conditions in the factory towns of Britain and weaning savage races away from their barbarous practices and converting them to Christianity. And there was no group of people anywhere who were more in need of being uplifted by Christianity and civilisation than the ever warring, Stone Age tribes of New Zealand.

In the words of the *Sydney Herald* of 22nd November, 1839, the Church Missionary Society "has managed successfully to pursue political objects in Downing Street to the extent, so far as respects New Zealand, of being a branch of the Colonial Office." The paper went on to describe "the influence of the Church Missionary Society and the Colonial Office bureaucracy on the feeble and faint-hearted government".[3]

Thus from the very beginning it was clear that London intended that the colonisation of this new and fertile land of great promise in the Temperate Zone (larger than the island of Great Britain) would be carried out with as few adverse effects as possible on the native population. Hence the Maoris were given a much better colonisation deal than had been the case with the Indians of North and South America, the natives in South Africa and the aborigines in Australia.

As John Robinson wrote in his book, *The Kohimarama Conference, 1860*, "It is important to recognise that this was to be a new, untried effort of humanitarian colonisation".[4] And Professor Keith Sinclair in his *History of New Zealand*, "These instructions [of Lord Normanby, the Colonial Secretary] marked a new and noble beginning in British colonial policy. The history of New Zealand was to be distinguished from that of earlier settlement colonies; the fate of the Maoris was to differ from that of the American Indian, the Bantu, the Australian or Tasmanian aborigine; for the new colony was being launched in an evangelical age. Imperialism and humanitarianism would henceforth march together".[5]

They certainly did, starting with Article Third of the Treaty of Waitangi, which granted to the Maoris (including the slaves) all the rights and privileges of British subjects - the first time that this favoured status was bestowed on a native race.

In the following pages we shall look at the impact on colonisation on the people and environment and see how this dynamic force worked to uplift the lives of the natives who, at the time of their first contact with Europeans (late 18th and early 19th centuries), had invented neither writing nor the wheel.

The only truthful way of assessing whether colonisation was a benefit or not is to look at how the natives were living pre-1840 and then see how far they advanced after coming into contact with new people, new ideas, new products and a new way of life. That they went through such an amazing transformation in so short a time and uplifted themselves in the process gives the natives cause for pride and all New Zealanders something to celebrate.

As John Robinson wrote in *When Two Cultures Meet. the New Zealand Experience,* "The New Zealand story is of successful and beneficial integration, with no colour bar and intermarriage from the first time of meeting." [6]

CHAPTER 2

FOOD

"The New Zealanders [natives] are a people who of all others are the least capable of bearing hunger with patience."

John Nicholas, *Narrative of a Voyage to New Zealand.* [1]

Before the arrival of Europeans the Maoris were existing on a limited range of food types - fish (kahawai, snapper, barracouta, dogfish, moki), shellfish, eels, birds (wild fowl, wood hens (weka), oyster catchers), kumera, taro, yams, and hu-hu grubs as well as berries and fern root. They would preserve some of these foods, plus dog (kuri) and the kiore rat. In addition to these, cannibalism was often used as a source of protein, especially by war parties. Slaves too could be a source of food whenever their owners felt like killing and eating them.

Fern root was more or less their daily sustenance whereas kumera - and later potatoes - were regarded more as an occasional luxury. They would dig, beat and roast the fern root and then chew it. "Being thus prepared for use, the cooks throw it [the fern root] round in handfuls to the chiefs and other persons, who chew it till all the sacharine or nutritive matter is extracted; and, spitting out the fibrous part, they go on again and continue in this manner till they have satisfied their appetites. The fern root, when hot, has a pleasant sweetish taste and, on being steeped in water, deposes a glutinous substance resembling jelly," noted the observant John Nicholas, who accompanied Rev. Samuel Marsden to New Zealand in 1814-15. [2]

War parties ate only fern root as it was the food of Tu, the god of war, "kumera and all other kinds of food are forbidden until the war is over". [3]

However, the constant gnawing of the tough roots of the fern as well as the gritty shellfish and other hard foods wore away the teeth so that by about the age of twenty the teeth at the back of the mouth were worn to stumps. [4] It didn't help that they also chewed the big stalks of the pampas grass (*toetoe*). "We invite all the sons of chiefs to come in; they must all enter and sit naked, leaving their clothes at some distance from the house. Everyone must bring in his hand a *toetoe* stalk pulled up by the roots so that when the old men have done teaching them, they may chew the lower end of the stalk, which will make their memories remember what they have heard," wrote John White in his book, *Te Rou, or the Maori at Home*, of a tribal gathering preparatory to going to war. [5]

"Early European observers such as Captain Cook frequently misjudged the age of Maoris as their toothless state made them appear much older than they were." [6] Needless to say, colonisation brought dental care as the first decades of the nineteenth century saw tremendous strides in the skills and knowledge of dentistry throughout the Western world. Part-Maoris of to-day, who have their teeth, have reason to be grateful for this aspect of colonisation, which lifted them out of a veritable dental disaster.

For cooking, the pre-European Maori favoured the underground *hangi* or the *umu* (an above ground oven of hot volcanic stones). True boiling of food was rare or impossible as they did not have the utensils to withstand the heat. However, tribes who lived near hot springs such as at Rotorua were able to boil food in the thermal pools.

The early Europeans in New Zealand also cooked outdoors - in pots and on spits suspended over wood-fuelled, open fires. However, it wasn't long before the colonists advanced to the Dutch or camp oven (a sturdy, lidded pot on legs) and also to the colonial oven, a cast iron box with doors, on top of which the fire was heaped.

All these required to be lit and here again the Maori benefited from the European inventions of the tinder box and also candles - a far cry from the pre-colonisation method of making fires (especially for cooking) which was the "fire plough" - rubbing a stick in a groove until the friction produced a spark. Later came the safety matches and then the cigarette lighter, requiring only the slight pressure of the thumb to bring a flame.

By the 1850s the even more advanced cast iron ranges were being imported from Britain and America and then in 1873 Henry Shacklock's famous Orion range hit the market in a big way. From there to the electric stoves and gas ovens of the 20th and 21st centuries - a huge advance for the Maoris in the important daily task of cooking.

One of the first European foods to be enjoyed by the Maori was the potato, which Captain Cook is believed to have introduced to the natives of Queen Charlotte Sound during his second voyage in 1773. The potato helped end the threat of food shortages for the tribes as its yield was far higher than that of the kumera and it took far less time to grow.

However, it could still take a lot of effort as John Nicholas observed in 1814. "While passing through some adjacent fields I saw some men and women busily engaged in digging up potatoes; and the instrument they used for the purpose was very rude and imperfect. This wretched substitute for a spade was a pole about seven feet long, terminating in a sharp point, and having at the distance of three feet from the extremity a piece of wood fastened at right angles as a rest for the foot." [7]

Similarly in building a trench. "While some were entrenching, others might be seen digging with all their might....Many looked like dogs scratching. Stooping half double, they threw the soil up with their hands out of the trench into the *pa*, where others beat the soil with sticks to form the rampart and to make it solid." [8] This was a Stone Age society, the definition of "Stone Age" being that their tools and weapons were made of stone and not metal. Indeed, the first time that these primitive people saw metal was when the sailors on Cook's *Endeavour* traded nails and fish hooks with them in return for food.

Whereas European people had been using metal since the Bronze Age and the Iron Age the Maoris of the late eighteenth century were still using stone tools for every task. "With rude and blunt stones they felled the giant kauri - toughest of pines; and from it in process of time, at an expense of labour, perseverance and ingenuity perfectly astounding to those who know what it really was, produced, carved, painted and inlaid a masterpiece of art and an object of beauty - the war canoe, capable of carrying a hundred men on a distant expedition". [9]

On his second voyage Captain Cook also planted at Ship Cove in the Queen Charlotte Sound wheat, peas, carrots, parsnips and strawberries, thus bringing these staples to New Zealand for the first time. However, he planted them primarily as a food source for his crew rather than for the natives.

As more Europeans arrived they brought with them their cows and sheep, pigs and poultry, milk and cream, fruit trees and honey bees. Cows and horses arrived on the *Active* with Rev. Samuel Marsden in 1814. In the words of John Nicholas, who was on board, "The cows and horses, animals they had never seen before, excited their surprise in a wonderful degree; and one of them, seeing a cow with her head stooping down, inquired with much earnestness in what part the mouth was." [10]

The natives were equally surprised when introduced to the horse, which they first saw when Rev. Marsden rode one along the beach in Northland. "To see a man seated on the back of such an animal, they thought the strangest thing in nature; and, following him with staring eyes, they believed at the moment that he was more than mortal," wrote Nicholas. [11]

Thus did colonisation bring a better and more varied diet for the native people and, to their credit, they embraced these new products, with tribes starting to grow a surplus of food so that they could trade it with settlers and other tribes. As a consequence some tribes became quite rich. This was possible only as a result of the peace that was brought to the warring tribes by the introduction of British law, thus ending the insecurity that deterred them from planting anything beyond their immediate needs on the grounds that a stronger tribe might displace them from their planting grounds before a crop could be picked.

Of particular benefit to the natives was the honey bee as the native bees of New Zealand did not pollinate the prolific manuka bushes that, with colonisation, were to provide them with honey. Beehives were brought out from Britain on the decks of the immigrant vessels. In recent times the successor race of part-Maoris now proclaim manuka honey as being "indigenous" and yet there would be no manuka honey without the introduction of honey bees and beehives by the colonists.

Pre-colonisation the Maoris' cultivation of kumera and taro was more in the nature of gardening than farming. It was the Europeans who introduced the concept of pastoral farming, with cattle, sheep, pigs, etc. Colonisation also brought about arable crop farming for the first time, with the European invented plough and harrow pulled by imported bullocks and later draught horses. These developments by the settlers ensured the best use of New Zealand's fertile land and has provided the bulk of the export income ever since, thus lifting the standard of living of all New Zealanders so that in the 1950s and 1960s we were at the very top of the standard of living statistics in comparison with other nations. This, unfortunately, is no longer the case.

The first plough arrived in New Zealand in 1819 and was used to break ground for wheat in the Bay of Islands. It was a single bladed plough but it had to wait for the arrival of ten bullocks on *HMS Dromedary* in March, 1820, before it could be used since it required six of the beasts to pull it. The *Dromedary* also brought the harnesses that enabled the quadrupeds to pull the plough. It was this humble plough that began the systematic cultivation of New Zealand. Soon five acres of wheat had sprung up at the Keirkeri Mission. [12]

1819 was also the year in which the first grape was planted in New Zealand by Rev. Samuel Marsden at the Kerikeri Mission - the beginning of the New Zealand wine industry. The grapes grew well. In the words of Edward Jerningham Wakefield, writing of a visit that he paid to Hokianga in 1840, "About two miles above Maungungu we found the establishment of Lieutenant Macdonnell...The fig and prickly pear were growing well in the open air, and a vineyard with 350 vines of different sorts promised great things". [13]

At Parihaka the self-proclaimed prophet, Te Whiti, used to hold feasts at his monthly meetings that in the 1870s and early 1880s were attended by around 2,000 natives. Even though Te Whiti was opposed to European ways the food that they all ate at these meetings was Western food and not their previous diet. For example, at the meeting in September, 1879, "Over 200 pigs were killed and four bullocks, a number of mutton-birds and several cart-loads of bread were also served out at the feast". [14] Again at the meeting in March, 1880, 50 pigs and 100 sheep were slaughtered for the plate as well as 200 large baskets of bread, 300 flax kits (bags) of melons, and 30 boxes of tea." [15]

Some tribes brought wheat to the meetings, which would have been threshed at one of the three threshing machines that Parihaka operated,[16] the threshing machines being yet another European invention that benefited the Maoris.

From Europeans the natives had learned how to grind and mill flour from the grain and it is to their credit that they created several varieties, e.g. Rewena bread, which was oven-baked and leavened with a "culture" (bug) made from the juice of boiled potato. They learned from the Europeans how to make butter by skimming the milk from the European introduced cows and then churning the cream into butter.

"The natives at Parihaka are very sullen and evidently desire no intercourse with Europeans," wrote the *Wanganui Herald* on 20th September, 1881. Maybe, but they couldn't get along without European introduced food, cutlery and plates. The European introduced potato was the main item of food at Parihaka - as it was in most Maori villages. Certainly an improvement on fern root. And not just the food; the natives who poured into Parihaka for these monthly meetings/feasts arrived for the most part on horses or in horse drawn carts, both being European introductions.

Pre colonisation the natives relied on a sharp piece of obsidian (a glassy volcanic rock) or the sharp edges of shells to cut food whereas colonisation brought all the utensils of the Victorian housewife or cook - iron pots and pans, metal knives, forks and spoons (usually made in

Sheffield, England) and much more. These were eagerly taken up by the natives.

In the matter of pottery, earthenware plates, cups, etc. were unknown to the Polynesians. They got by with vessels made of wood or basketry - and occasionally stone. Baskets mostly served as the dish for eating. Before being introduced to European cups and glasses for drinking they put the water, etc. into the trough of their hand(s) and slurped it.

The sharp edges of shells were also used at lamentations where "the women sing the dismal dirge, cutting their faces and lacerating their breasts with sharp shells, till covered with blood". [17]

In the words of Captain John Hemery, who brought the *Bengal Merchant* into Wellington harbour in February, 1840, with the first Scottish settlers for New Zealand on board, "The natives are the most warlike and independent set of savages I ever saw. They are very fine, tall men, all tattooed over the face and body, which gives them a fearful appearance. They are continually at war with each other but the tribe in this neighbourhood are quite friendly to the whites. They [the natives] are exceedingly sensitive of any affront or injury and very quick at avenging it. They are also very selfish and grasping....... barter is chiefly carried on with blankets, although they begin to talk of gold and silver quite naturally.....A hostile tribe came down here the other night and got hold of a Chief whose heart they cut out and whose head they cut off and ran away with". This was Puakawa, who was beheaded in his potato patch on the Hutt River by a foraging party of Ngati kahunu.

To honour the dead chief the natives had a wake, which was witnessed by Captain Hemery. "The whole tribe was making the most dreadful noise I ever heard, making the most horrid faces, sticking their tongues out of their mouths and barking and growling like wolves. The next awful performances were the women, who kept cutting their bodies and faces with shells. Some of them were one mass of blood all over the body and I don't think there were four inches of them without a deep gash which they had inflicted with a sharp part of the shell". [18]

F.E. Maning observed one of these shows when a group of women were wailing over a severed head "and cutting themselves dreadfully with sharp flints and shells. One old woman, in the centre of the group, was one clot of blood from head to feet, and large clots of coagulated blood lay on the ground where she stood. The sight was absolutely horrible.....In her right hand she held a piece of *tuhua*, or volcanic glass, as sharp as a razor; this she placed deliberately to her left wrist, drawing it slowly upwards to her left shoulder, the spouting blood following as it went, and from the left shoulder downwards, across the breast to the short ribs on the right side. She then shifted the rude but keen knife from the right hand to the left, placed it to the right wrist, drawing it upwards to the right shoulder and so down across the breast to the left side, thus making a bloody cross on the breast. And so the operation went on all the time I was there, the old creature all the time howling in time and measure....She had scored her forehead and cheeks before I came; her face and body were one mass of blood and a little stream was dropping from every finger." [19]

Another part of the pre-colonisation diet was the native dog - "a numerous and ugly species" according to Captain Cook. [20] "There are numbers of dogs running wild....but I could not discover that they ever offered any injury to the inhabitants, who prize them very highly, as well for the sake of their flesh, which serves them for a delicious article of food," wrote John Nicholas. [21]

So too had the moa before it was killed and eaten to extinction - all nine species of them so that by the time Captain Cook arrived there was not a single one of these great birds left. "At times the killing of the moa assumed an almost industrial scale", wrote W.F. Benfield in his book, *The Third Wave; Poisoning the Land*. [22] Some of the killing sites were so rich in moa bones that, after colonisation, railway wagons had to be used to remove them and convert them into fertiliser. "It was a blitzkrieg of butchery. If it was there, it was destroyed. It wasn't only moa. It was also the easily harvested bird life, the kakapo, the adzbill, the flightless geese and ducks; even the flighted black swan". [23]

Another part of their diet was whales - at least in the whaling areas. "We again observed the wretched appearance of the houses and food of the natives. Much of the latter consisted of dried whale's flesh, of which we saw large quantities hung on racks about the village", wrote Edward Jerningham Wakefield after a visit to a whaling station in Queen Charlotte Sound. [24]

The healthier and more varied diet introduced by the colonists, including the meat of animals instead of the meat of people, has been of inestimable value to the natives and their descendants, with the life expectancy of Maoris tripling from 20 to 25 years (1840) to 77.1 years for women and 73.4 years for men in 2019. So, in respect of food, its preparation and cooking, and the utensils for eating it, colonisation has been a big benefit.

CHAPTER 3

CLOTHING

When the Polynesians arrived in New Zealand in the thirteenth century they had come from sub-tropical islands where very little clothing was required, and they could keep relatively clean by bathing in the warm lagoons of the atolls. But New Zealand is much colder and it was harder for them to keep their bodies warm. The chiefs kept themselves warm with thick cloaks made of dogskin and feathers but those of lesser rank - both men and women - generally had to make do with garments or mats made of woven flax that covered the shoulders, hips and sometimes the knees.

Some of them "were fancifully worked round with variegated borders, and decorated in other respects". [1] Some of the mats were "dyed with red ochre so that the appearance they presented was gay and characteristic". [2]

However, when Rev. J. Buller arrived at Hokianga in 1835 he noted, "They [the natives] were clothed in rough mats or in dirty blankets." [3] As late as the 1870s and 1880s Te Whiti would address his meetings at Parihaka wearing only a dirty blanket but this seems to have been done for public relations purposes (a cloak of victimhood) as, like all cult leaders, Te Whiti was a rich man who extracted large donations from his followers in both cash and kind.

However, flax is a light material and not particularly warm. This is probably the explanation for fossil evidence showing that pre-European Maori suffered greatly from arthritis. Flax had been used for thousands of years in other parts of the world (Mesopotamia, Greece, etc.) and from it linen was created. However, the Maoris never made this advance themselves despite the abundance of flax. Even the Stone Age people of New Guinea managed to make cloth from flax fibre.

For rainwear pre-European Maori used a rain cloak called *pake* or *hieke*. It was made from tags of raw flax, partly scraped and set in close rows attached to the *muka* or plaited fibre base.

Of footwear they knew nothing. The first shoes and boots they saw were on the feet of Captain Cook and his sailors. Even after the arrival of settlers the Maoris were known as "the bare-footed people". Their feet must have been very tough as they sometimes walked dozens and hundreds of miles through the bush to make war on other tribes.

With the coming of European traders and settlers Maoris were able to purchase warm woollen clothing as well as a plethora of headwear, footwear and water-proof coats and jackets. The everyday dress of the pioneer European settlers, that came to be adopted by the natives, consisted of working clothes - moleskin trousers, cotton shirt and neckcloth for the men and long dresses over petticoats and poke bonnets for the women.

However, the transition was not always smooth. In the words of the missionary, Rev. W. Yate, "At times they cut a most grotesque appearance in their new clothing as how many articles soever a man may possess, he will frequently manage to have them all on at once. His trousers perhaps will be tied round his neck, his shirt put on as trousers, his jacket the wrong way before or turned inside out. The women, if they happen to have two or three gowns, will put them all on; and they will manage so to arrange their dress as to have some part of each article visible." [4]

European clothing was most welcome. In the words of Thomas Kempton, who arrived in Wellington on the *Adelaide* in March, 1840, and engaged a couple of natives to help him build a house of clay and wood with long grass for the thatch of the roof, "I gave them each a shirt for payment. They were very pleased at the price for at this time there were many of them who went naked and very savage in their appearance." [5]

As late as 1849, when *HMS Acheron* was in Queen Charlotte Sound during her marine surveying trip around the New Zealand coast, it seems that some of the natives were still short of warm clothing. "Being mostly ill-clad, they seemed to feel the cold much, and earnestly begged permission that they might light their pipes and warm themselves at the galley fire," wrote the diarist of the *Acheron*. [6]

The people of early New Zealand - natives and settlers - owe a debt to the Scottish chemist, Charles Mackintosh, who in the 1820s invented the waterproof material for raincoats that bears his name - the mackintosh or mac. The fabric was made waterproof by cementing two thicknesses of it together with rubber dissolved in a coal-tar naphtha solution, naphtha being a by-product of tar.

Another invention, the sewing machine, was a huge advance on the Maori woman's only known method of hand stitched weaving. In the 1880s Singer sewing machines, invented by the American, Isaac Merritt Singer, started entering New Zealand. They had foot-powered treadles and by the 1880s and 1890s they were being widely used in households as well as in tailoring and dressmaking businesses.

Writing of the early years of colonisation, Rev. William Williams stated, "A very few years brought about a vast change in their [the natives'] general appearance and pursuits. English clothing superseded the native garment". [7] Of a young Maori chap whom he saw riding a horse in the 1860s Judge F.E. Maning wrote, "he wore a black hat and polished Wellingtons, his hat was cocked knowingly to one side and he was jogging along with one hand jingling the money in his pocket". [8]

Even pocket watches. When John Nicholas visited Northland in 1814 with Samuel Marsden he wrote, "But my watch was a much more pleasing spectacle....Everyone was impatient to have a peep at it but the ticking was so wonderful to their conceptions that they believed it to be nothing less than the language of a god; and the watch itself..... was regarded by the whole of them with profound reverence". [9]

This "god" was soon to be used by them as an article of clothing, e.g. Tamihana Te Rauparaha, the son of the old cannibal chief, was photographed wearing an English suit with a pocket watch. This

European contrivance gave the natives the ability to tell the time, something that they had hitherto been unable to do apart from looking at the position of the sun. This accoutrement was certainly an improvement on their pre-colonisation personal decoration of wearing around their necks a string of teeth from an eaten enemy. Thus from so many angles in the matter of clothing, colonisation was a very big plus for the native people.

CHAPTER 4

HOUSING

"By no stretch of the imagination can the *whare* [native house] be viewed as a comfortable place," wrote Elsdon Best [1] who described the housing that he saw as mere "huts" (about twelve feet long and four to five feet high). Sometimes the doorways were so low that people had to crawl through them. The native hut lacked a chimney and ventilation for the fires that were sometimes lit inside them in cold weather, thus producing a lot of unhealthy smoke in this sleeping place. Many of them were infested with vermin.

In the words of John Nicholas, who visited a *pa* in Northland in 1814, "We came to a little village consisting of fourteen huts. Our curiosity was at once excited to see the inmates but none were to be found as they had all fled to an adjacent wood and left the huts quite deserted on our approach. The poor creatures were struck with terror at the idea that we were come to kill them, and forsook their miserable dwellings through the impulse of this groundless alarm.

The huts were constructed on a very simple plan, and had evidently a greater regard to room than to convenience; indeed, nothing of the latter description was at all to be seen. They all appeared much of the same dimensions and were generally about fourteen feet in length and eight in breadth but the height was never more than four. The buildings were composed of sticks and reeds (*toetoe*) interwoven with each other, but so very imperfectly and with such little care to guard against the changes of the weather, that the appearance was extremely wretched. Windows were never thought of, and the hole which was intended for a door was so very low and narrow that it required them to crawl on their hands and knees in order to squeeze themselves in and out through it". [2] Yet some of the natives were "six feet and upwards, and all their limbs were remarkable for perfect symmetry and great muscular strength". [3]

The walls of the structures were none too sturdy. One man wanted to see what was going on inside a big house where a white man was being entertained but he was not allowed to enter through the door because he had just come from a kumera field that was *tapu* and so he was believed to carry the curse with him. So as not to be left out of the proceedings he made a hole with his fist in the padded raupo wall and squeezed his head through it, thus beating the *tapu* which prevented him going through the door. [4]

"The floor was covered with dry grass, over which were mats made of the flax leaf, split into shreds and plaited," wrote John White in *Te Rou, or the Maori at Home*. [5] Very different from the woollen carpets of today, made from the wool of the sheep that the colonists introduced to these verdant islands.

Life in the *pa* was communal, in fact communistic. The European concepts of a family unit (mother, father and children) and the privacy of the home were unknown to traditional Maori. Gradual acceptance of "compartmentalised" housing brought the Maori family together for the first time.

During a visit to the Marlborough Sounds in 1840 Edward Jerningham Wakefield wrote, "We found the village of Anaho in a level piece of ground at the head of Cannibal Cove, and were much amused by seeing the *whare puni,* or sleeping houses, of the natives. These are exceedingly low, and covered with earth on which weeds very often grow.....A small square hole at one end is the only passage for light and air. I intended to creep into one of them to examine it but had just got my head in and was debating within myself by what snake-like evolution I should best succeed in getting my body to follow, when I was deterred by the intense heat and intolerable odour from proceeding". [6]

Further down the South Island the floors of the huts were dug into the ground to a depth of about two feet. This was to keep them warm in the freezing southern climes. With the onslaught of colonisation their conditions steadily improved and now their descendants are kept warm in the winter by such Western inventions as central heating and electric blankets.

And not just warmth but security as well; before colonisation no native could go to bed without fearing that he or she might be attacked during the night - and maybe killed and eaten - by a stronger tribe from across the hills or over the water. It was the introduction of British law in 1840 that put an end to such fears.

A chief would usually inhabit a larger house, called a *whare kopae*, but, no matter what the size, Maori dwellings were never divided into rooms. Of one chief's hut John Nicholas wrote, "The hut of this chief....differed but little from those of his subjects, and was distinguished only by its being built upon a larger scale and having more ground enclosed around it. It measured about twenty feet long, fifteen broad, and eight feet in height, with a ridge-like roof, and built of sticks interwoven with rushes.....The interior presented nothing to compensate the trouble of getting in, and a few stones thrown together to serve for a fire-place were the only domestic articles I could possibly discover. Furniture was none and, the smoke finding no egress except through the doorway, which was the only aperture to be seen, the dismal edifice teemed with suffocating vapour and formed, with the wretched inmates, a complete picture of cheerless barbarism". [7]

"No people had less in the way of furniture than the Maori folk", observed Elsdon Best. "In fact, save mats, they had none, and the interior of the house or hut was bare and comfortless from our point of view....These people used no form of raised seat, and no form of table". [8]

The natives never ate their meals in their huts - even if it was raining. During the time when a native was building or repairing his hut he was under *tapu* (quarantine), a requirement of which was that he was not allowed to feed himself. For a chief, people would have to feed him with his hands tied behind his back, but for a commoner the meal was just left for him and he had to stoop down and try to take it into his mouth as best he could without using his hands - all out of fear of their god, Etua. This rather cruel practice was ended with the introduction of Christianity.

As colonisation proceeded, the Maoris began to build or buy European style wooden bungalows with the various conveniences of the Victorian period. In 1881 Te Whiti of Parihaka built for himself a nice, European styled wooden house, neatly painted, with three bedrooms and muslin curtains over the windows. He might have railed against the European presence in New Zealand but he couldn't live without its comforts.

It was the British scientist, Michael Faraday, who invented electricity in 1831 and in New Zealand this new wonder was first used at Reefton in 1888, giving it street lighting and other benefits.

Electricity changed the lives of all New Zealanders - settler and native - beyond all recognition, providing light at all times of the day and night through the light bulb, heating and cooling homes, refrigerating food, and cooking it when required. The comparison between the smoky, unfurnished hut of the early Maori, lit, if it was, by three torches of pine bark "stuck up in the centre", [9] and the modern, European style houses in which part-Maori live to-day could not be starker and is further evidence of the benefits of colonisation to the Maori.

CHAPTER 5

TRANSPORT

Before contact with the wider world of the European the only mode of land transport that the Maoris had was to walk through the bush in their bare feet, breaking off twigs and branches with their hands as they went so as to make or maintain tracks. They had no horses or any similar animal to ride and nor had they invented the wheel - something that had been invented as early as 3,500 B.C. and was, by the eighteenth century, in wide use in other places and continents. After it was brought to New Zealand by the British, the wheel enabled Maoris to learn to ride, using horse and cart, and then the bicycle, the car, the truck, the motor bike, agricultural machinery and all the rest.

The sea travel of the pre-contact Maoris was more advanced in the form of their great war canoes, which could travel swiftly, enabling aggressive and hungry tribes like Ngapuhi to go down from the Bay of Islands to attack tribes in the Bay of Plenty, and Te Rauparaha and his fellow cannibals of Ngati Toa to cross Cook Strait to kill, cook and eat the South Island tribes.

In their sea travel the Maoris used the stars for navigation but, with the arrival of European know-how, they were introduced to the magnetic compass, which had been used by European seafarers ever since the Vikings rowed their great vessels across the North Sea and elsewhere in their piratical and colonising undertakings. The compass made it easier for the Maoris in their sea and river expeditions as well as trips through the dense bush.

The first road in New Zealand, running for a mile and a quarter at Whangaroa in Northland, was built in 1820 by the sailors of *HMS Dromedary*, which ship we met in the Food chapter, and the troops of the 84th Regiment who were also on board. Having deposited her consignment of 369 convicts at Sydney, the ship came on to New

Zealand to take on kauri spars (in her case 98) so that they could be fitted as topmasts for the Navy's sailing vessels in the Naval Dockyards in England. Each mast had to be between 74 and 84 feet in length, and 21 to 23 inches in diameter and perfectly straight.

The purpose of the road which the troops and sailors built was to drag kauri logs over it from a ravine on the Mangaiti Stream, a tributary of the Kaeo River. From there they could be floated out to the *Dromedary* and hauled on board. They were dragged along the road by ten bullocks that the ship had taken on board in Sydney.

This road, the forerunner of thousands more to come with colonisation, took several months to build. It included a bridge over the Mangaiti Stream strong enough to take the weight of the bullocks and their load. In the words of one of the *Dromedary's* officers, Richard Cruise, "It is scarcely possible to imagine that so small a number of people, with such inadequate means, could have effected an undertaking apparently so far beyond their powers." [1]

New Zealand's second road, a ten mile route which involved the construction of three bridges, was made in 1831 between Kerikeri and Waimate, the inland site of the Church Missionary Society. Its purpose was to convey stores from the water at Kerikeri to the Mission.

After the first settlers arrived at Wellington in 1840 it was clear that the badly maintained Maori foot tracks were not fit for purpose and so the energetic settlers set about building tracks (roads) for pedestrians and horses, later widened to take bullocks and carts. The first of these was the Hutt Road, connecting the original settlement at Petone with the later one on the shore of Lambton harbour. The work was done by the pioneers, including those Scots who arrived on the *Blenheim* on 27 December, 1840, and were accommodated in barracks at Kaiwharawhara and soon set to work with picks and wide-mouth shovels.

Upon completion of the Hutt Road the ever enterprising New Zealand Company drove a track through the thick bush to the north-west, to link Wellington with Porirua harbour which, before the earthquake of

1855, was navigable to small vessels and schooners for a considerable distance.

As settlement expanded outwards from the mother settlement of Wellington more and more roads were built, including the difficult Otira road to connect Christchurch with the newly discovered gold fields on the West Coast, and the Great South Road which penetrated south from Auckland into the thickly forested Waikato.

With its abundance of high mountains and raging rivers taking high country rain to the ocean, there was a need for bridges all over the place - mostly small wooden structures that were not all that high out of the water. So as not to impede boat traffic going up river these bridges often had a swing-span that could be activated to turn it around 90 degrees to let a vessel through. The first swing-span bridge seems to have been the Heathcote Bridge in Christchurch (completed 1864) and the second, the Panmure Bridge at Auckland (completed 1865).

Some rivers were deemed "unbridgeable", which was a challenge to the skills of the engineers and contractors, e.g. the long bridge across the Rakaia River in Canterbury, built by William White, which was opened in 1873.

The Vogel Public Works Act of 1870 spread the iron tracks of the railway across much of the country, requiring numerous tunnels, viaducts and bridges. The bulk of the work (surveying, digging, blasting with dynamite (invented by the Swede, Alfred Nobel, in 1867), plate-laying, etc.) was done by the pioneer settlers, with no convict labour (as in Australia) and very little native labour.

Large amounts of capital were required for these projects and this was invariably raised on the London capital market, with some of the companies such as the Midland Railway Company, which tried to put the railway through from Canterbury to the West Coast, and the Auckland Electric Tramway Company, being entirely British affairs with British shareholders. New Zealand was fortunate to have been colonised by the British when England was at the height of its power and achievements in the Industrial Revolution, which had made

Britain the richest country ever known to history at that time. Hence the availability of capital for all the required infrastructure not only for New Zealand but for much of the world. New Zealand owes much to the institutions in Britain that trained the engineers and the firms that gave them their experience before they boarded a smelly, crowded sailing ship for the four to five months voyage to the Antipodes where they applied their skills with such success.

Sea travel was made safer and easier by the naval surveying of the coast by *HMS Acheron* and *HMS Pandora* between 1848 and 1855, and by the construction of numerous wharves, docks for repairing ships, and lighthouses. The new maps and charts of New Zealand's coast, estuaries and rivers that were the products of this great marine survey, carried out by the skilled surveyors of the Royal Navy, gave Maoris their first understanding of the shape and make-up of what had become their country out of the shambles of the inter-tribal wars.

Everybody in New Zealand benefited from this massive building of infrastructure which, in a mere sixty years from 1840, transformed the country from "trackless wastes to a well-serviced nation ('from Sone Age to Space Age')". [2] Apart from a few recalcitrants the bulk of the Maori population embraced these changes which brought them greater ease and comfort in getting from one place to another - horses, carts, trains, and then passenger liners and motor cars - a far cry from their earlier picking their way through the bush with bare, horny feet.

The twentieth century saw the arrival of the Western invented aeroplane for both carrying passengers and topdressing. This too was a far cry from the kite flying (*pakau*) of the early Maori when they used flax and bark to make the things fly in the wind. This was the limit of Maori invention in respect of the sky.

CHAPTER 6

HYGIENE

"In pre-European times the Maori lived in much the same manner as apparently did the neolithic folk of Britain, in communities the size of which was controlled by the food supply".

Elsdon Best, *The Maroi As He Was.* [1]

Pre-European Maori had a primitive system of hygiene and latrines in their villages, which were alive with rats and vermin. During his visit to New Zealand with Samuel Marsden in 1814-5 John Nicholas noted, "These people were so very dirty in their persons that any contact with them was truly disgusting. I do believe they had never been washed from the hour of their birth up to the moment we beheld them; and that species of loathsome vermin to which uncleanly Europeans have so long been familiarised, were crawling all over them in myriads." [2]

When Nicholas was being rowed back to his ship, the *Active*, by some native oarsmen he noticed one of them "apply his hand to his head very frequently, and then thrust his fingers into his mouth; while his filthy purpose being no longer doubtful, I soon discovered that he was feasting himself on the swarms of vermin he had engendered, and that his dirty head was a regular resource to his more dirty stomach.....It is strange why these people, who are extremely exact in some other respects, should be so shockingly disgusting in this; for, though their plantations are neatly laid out and their huts kept in tolerable order, their persons are suffered to swarm with cootoos [vermin], which it would seem they rather wish to encourage than expel." [3]

Observing these in 1840, Edward Jerningham Wakefield wrote of "the miserable appearance of the native villages......Crowded together, as the natives were, in small, filthy and unwholesome huts, we found that the animal heat, unpurified by ventilation, forced them to sleep quite naked, and that both sexes and all ages lay thus huddled together like dormice in a nest." [4]

Of the native *pa* at Te Aro, Wellington, he wrote, "Consisting entirely of low, miserable thatched sheds, with fires inside and no chimneys, leaning against dry, wooden fences, these inhabited dunghills are dangerous to themselves and to the rest of the town in case of accident by fire. They harbour troops of half-starved, mangy mongrels which rush out day and night upon every horse and foot passenger." [5]

The Maori *pa* had a "public toilet" - usually at the edge of the village - which all members of the *pa* used. But not always as John Nicholas noted in 1815 when some natives came aboard the *Active* and one of them performed "in the cabin, without any ceremony, one of the offensive offices of nature, while we were at dinner, for which he was immediately turned out". [6] On this occasion some chiefs had crowded into the cabin of the *Active*, which forced Marsden and Nicholas to quit it rather than "remain confined among them to experience the stench emitted from their dirty persons". [7]

The missionaries and the medics did their best to wean the natives away from such unhealthy habits but they were up against the *tohungas* (native priests) who resisted anything that they thought might threaten their powers and the superstitions of the people.

As late as 1881 the *Taranaki Herald* reported that "the natives of Parihaka are in a deplorable state......They are fearfully affected with vermin, which has been induced by the crowded state of the *whares* and the want of cleanliness. Parihaka is absolutely filthy for want of sanitary precautions". [8]

A big step forward for Maori hygiene was the passing of the Tohunga Suppression Act 1907, a statute that had been formulated and promoted by all the Maori Members of Parliament at the time, including Maui Pomare (a medical doctor), Sir James Carroll and Sir Apirana Ngata, because of the damage that many *tohunga* teachings were doing to Maori health. These M.P.s appreciated the benefits of Western hygiene and medicine and were determined to put an end to the shenanigans of the *tohungas* once and for all. As John Robinson wrote in *Twisting the Treaty*, "Maori *tohunga* 'health' knowledge prior to European settlement was highly likely to kill the patient." [8]

The development of hygiene and its salutary effect on the health of Maoris was indeed a substantial benefit of colonisation. To-day part-Maoris can wash their bodies with soap and their hair with shampoo - both introduced to New Zealand by the European settlers.

Women preparing land for a kumera patch. Women and slaves generally did the hard physical work.

A tohunga being fed by a young girl. See Page 24.

Slaves digging a potato patch with a wooden spade. See Page 11.

A fortified native village.

How the bare-footed natives travelled before colonisation.

Hongi Hika, who travelled to England in 1820 and bought muskets in Sydney on the way home, was the one who instigated the Musket Wars, which over the ensuing two decades killed approximately one third of the Maori people - one of the highest proportions of genocide ever recorded.

Captain Cook's HMS Resolution in Dusky Sound, Fiordland, in 1773. It was here that the Great Navigator brewed some "spruce beer" with leaves and small branches of rimu and manuka, which were mixed with molasses (a type of treacle). See page 115.   From an oil painting by R. Bianchi.

CHAPTER 7

HEALTH

"Native knowledge of medicine may be described as non-existent in former times," wrote the historian, Elsdon Best. "No attempt was made to study it because it was believed that sickness and disease were caused by *atua* (evil spirits)".

"When a priest is required to cure a stomach ache, we know that it is an evil spirit gnawing the person's stomach; and to make him depart, we point with our fingers to the seat of pain and say:

> 'My stomach;
> My stomach;
> Sufficient stomach;
> Gnawing stomach, sufficient.'
> This makes the evil spirit depart". [1]

Such was the state of medical knowledge of these Stone Age people.

One of the worst failings, based on superstition and enforced by the wretched *tohungas*, was to abandon the sick and the dying into some outhouse away from the huts, as it was believed that to die in a normal hut would thereby make that hut *tapu* (forbidden). "So, in order to save the house for future use, when death was expected the sick man would be taken to an open shed". [2] Here the dying person was effectively abandoned by being under a *tapu* "and not to be approached till the Etua (*atua*) was pleased to deliver him from his sufferings by putting an end to his existence." [3]

In the words of the Church of England missionary, Rev. William Williams, the friends of the dying person "prohibited every kind of food from being given to them, water only being allowed. Thus the poor sufferer was literally starved to death." [4]

When F.E. Maning went to visit a dying native friend, "The old man I saw at once was at his last hour. He had dwindled to a mere skeleton. No food of any kind had been prepared for or offered to him for three days; as he was dying it was, of course, considered unnecessary." [5]

When Chief Duaterra was dying in 1815 both Samuel Marsden and John Nicholas sought to visit him but they were told that Etua was preying upon his entrails and that the chief would be killed as soon as these were devoured. "This notion, much more than the complaint under which they [the dying] labour, accelerates the death of sick people in New Zealand," opined John Nicholas. [6]

"So strongly is it impressed upon the minds of their friends that, when the symptoms appear at all dangerous, they think any sort of remedy would be impious and.....they never once murmur against the mystical vulture who gnaws them away according to his appetite." [7]

"Many a poor sufferer who, with a little ordinary attention, might be soon restored to health and vigour, is devoted by this horrid superstition to perish in the very midst of his kindred without a single effort being made for his recovery. But his death is not the only loss which the community sustains at the time it happens; his wife, though she durst not administer that simple aid which might have rescued him from a premature grave, is obliged to immolate herself at his dissolution, as an indispensable test of her faithful attachment".[8] A cruel, horrible and often unnecessary way to die. So different from the way of death for the natives' descendants in the 21st century when they enjoy free health care in a modern hospital with all the latest equipment and medication for lessening pain and extending life.

It was the early Protestant missionaries who first introduced the natives to health care and Western medicine but it was an uphill struggle. In the 1840s a sub-tribe of about 40 people "removed their *kainga* [village] from a dry, healthy position to the edge of a raupo swamp. I happened to be at the place a short time after the removal, and with me there was a medical gentleman who was travelling through the country. In creeping into one of the houses (the chief's) through the low door, I was obliged to put both my hands to the ground. They both sank into the swampy soil, making holes which immediately filled with water. The chief and his family were lying on the ground on rushes and a fire was burning, which made the little den, not in the highest place more than five feet high, feel like an oven. I called the attention of my friend to the state of this place called a 'house'. He merely said, 'men cannot live here'. Eight years from that day the whole *hapu* were extinct", wrote F.E. Maning. [9]

In the 1840s a small number of hospitals were set up by the colonial authorities specifically for Maoris to be treated with Western medicine. Subsidised "native medical officers" gave free treatment. "Improvement in health came first to those Maori who had the greatest contact with Europeans, and it spread steadily throughout the nineteenth century." [10]

Many of the natives suffered from sore eyes. They had difficulty opening them until the missionary, Thomas Kendall, started curing them by using goulard. It was believed that the prevalence of sore eyes was caused by their sleeping so often in the open air, under sometimes heavy dews and with their heads uncovered.

In the course of time the natives were introduced to European glasses, which one tribe saw for the first time on the face of John Nicholas in 1814. "The sight of my spectacles appeared to divert them exceedingly, and they were much puzzled to know for what use they could be intended. On my telling them that I could *tickee tickee nue nue* (see very far) with them, they immediately wished to make the experiment themselves and were extremely anxious to put them on; but with this curiosity I did not think it prudent to comply as I knew that the indulgence would only make them troublesome and importunate". [11]

Very wise for, in his own words, "The New Zealanders are, of all the people I ever met with, the most importunate in their demands upon strangers, and some of them are of so covetous a disposition that, give them what you will, they are not to be satisfied".[12] This is an interesting comment in view of the behaviour of the tribal elite in the 21st century who, having been given more than $3 billion of taxpayers' money in so-called "treaty settlements", still bleat for more.

Over the generations since colonisation many Maoris have been able to extend their optical powers by wearing European invented glasses, including the co-leader of the Maori Party, Rawiri Waititi, who, despite ranting against colonisation and its effects at every turn, wears glasses on his own ink-stained face, thus making himself an object of both ridicule and hypocrisy.

As time went on advances in medical knowledge in Europe and North America were passed on to New Zealand, whose doctors up until the middle of the 20th century usually did their learning and training in Britain - especially at Edinburgh University. A huge step forward was the invention of the X-ray by Wilhelm Rontgen in Germany in 1895. Much better than the *atua* of the primitive Maori.

As already stated, with the introduction of Western medicine the life expectancy of Maoris rose from 20 to 25 years (1840) to 76.5 years for women and 72.8 years for men in 2012. As they say in law, *res ipsa loquitur* (the thing speaks for itself).

CHAPTER 8

SUPERSTITION

"They had been trained up in gross superstition, and there did not appear to them any sufficient reason to abandon it......If their crops of kumara failed, the reason was that some ceremony at the time of planting had been neglected; and the privation suffered by the loss of the crop made them more careful for the future. Sickness was generally attributed to witchcraft, practised by a chief of some hostile tribe, or by an unfortunate slave, whose life was sure to be forfeited. The person of a leading chief was always sacred. His head, his garments, the ground upon which he sat, the remains of the food he had eaten, were all highly tabooed, and his people carefully avoided them, lest some evil should befall them", wrote Rev. Williams in his book, *Christianity Among the New Zealanders.* [1]

The native priests (*tohunga*), like the witchdoctors in Africa, exercised a sinister influence - the "limbs of Satan" as F.E. Maning called them.[2] "They were supposed to possess the power of bewitching whom they pleased, and hence they were much feared by the whole community. Their art was properly the black art and, in the education given to a person who was afterwards to hold the office, pains were taken to increase the disposition for evil". [3]

Some of these Stone Age people were so simple minded that they believed that they were descended from a mountain. In 1842, when Edward Jerningham Wakefield was visiting the centre of the North Island, he asked the local chief, Heuheu, if he (Wakefield) could climb Mount Tongariro. The chief refused, saying "You must not ascend my *tipuna*, or ancestor". [4]

As Wakefield pointed out, "This legend of an hereditary descent from an object, majestic in itself and naturally productive of awe....was wisely calculated to maintain the aristocratic position of the leader by appealing to the weak and superstitious imaginations of the crowd.....

Any visit made to the spot would, of course, be calculated to lessen the mystery, as the natives would soon learn from the white man that none of the danger existed which they supposed." [5]

This sort of nonsense was resurrected in 2010 when one of New Zealand's more stupid judges, Joanna Maze, fined a helicopter pilot $3,750 for hovering over the peak of Mount Cook, thus causing "cultural offence" to Ngai Tahu. In the summary of facts read to the court the Department of Conservation said that the peak of the mountain represented to Ngai Tahu "the most sacred of ancestors from whom Ngai Tahu descend and who provide the *iwi* with its sense of communal identity".[6] As Dr. Don Brash wrote in the book, *One Treaty; One Nation,* "If anybody in New Zealand actually does believe they are descended from a mountain, our education system is failing even more seriously than I had imagined." [7]

The primitive Maori were fixated on *tapu* (taboo). "In New Zealand, as in other countries where the people are utter strangers to the first principles of knowledge, the grossest delusions prevail, and the word taboo very frequently decides the actions of a whole race......It serves them in the absence of laws as the only security for the protection of persons and property, giving them an awful sacredness which no one dares to violate.....This superstition serves in a great measure to consolidate the limited power of the *arikis* over the inferior chiefs.... the *tohunga* or priest is the arbiter of all their delusions......The New Zealanders make no idols, nor have they any external form of worship; their conceptions of a supreme power being shewn only in the veneration they have for the above-mentioned superstition, and in the single word taboo all their religion and morality may be said to consist." [8]

Taboo extended to the moveable property (clothes, weapons, tools, etc) of the chiefs and petty chiefs and even to that of Europeans. As late as 1882, when the public works contractor, "Big" John McLean, was building a bridge across the Waipa River in the Waikato at Alexandra (now known as Pirongia), he was warned by the suspicious settlers there "that he would not be able to keep a tool or a piece of loose timber on the ground as it would be stolen by the natives". [9] He went straight to Tawhiao, the local chief who had led the 1860s rebellion in the Waikato, and had a pow-wow with him that lasted several hours. As a result Tawhiao was convinced that the bridge would be of value to the Maoris and he ordered Wahanui, one of his chiefs, to accompany the contractor to the site where, on Tawhiao's orders, he placed a *tapu* on all the materials and tools, thereby making them forbidden temptations so that no Maori would dare to steal them.

Throughout the entire contract John McLean never lost a single article. If a tool was accidentally mislaid or forgotten on a Saturday and the natives found it, they would bring it along unsolicited on the Monday morning and present it to the big Highlander. At the end of the contract he was able to say that he had never been more honestly dealt with than at Alexandra by Tawhiao and his people.

"An infringement of it (*tapu*) subjected the offender to various dreadful imaginary punishments, of which deadly sickness was one," wrote F.E. Maning.[10] This was how chiefs and other leaders such as Te Whiti and Tohu at Parihaka maintained their authority over their credulous followers. Te Whiti claimed to have supernatural powers, including the power to bring about death. In other words, "Don't mess with me".

A relative of Te Whiti's, Pihana, had been appointed by the Government as a Native Assessor at Parihaka - much to Te Whiti's annoyance. When Pihana later fell from his horse and died, Te Whiti tried to take credit for his death. "At a large meeting on Saturday....Te Whiti made a capital speech out of the accident, and quoted the case as an example of his miraculous power and the evil which will befall natives who worked against him." [11]

"The Maoris not only had faith in Te Whiti as a man able to do them good but they feared him, and particularly they feared Tohu....This was no trifling feeling.....it has been a feeling far exceeding in its intensity the ordinary fear of death", wrote the *Otago Daily Times* on 9th November, 1881. "Their faith that Te Whiti can ever become the ruler of the country, or can make the Maoris the dominant race, has faded or has gone; the expectation that he will achieve any good thing for them has almost left their thoughts; but the horrible dread of being '*maketu-ed*' (evil eye) bewitched or bedevilled to death is an ever present fear. They adhere to Te Whiti and obey him because they dare not do otherwise." [12]

Such fears often led a person to commit suicide in order to escape the fate that the *tohungas* predicted for him or her if they broke a *tapu* or for some other superstitious reason. "Suicides - in consequence of wounded pride, or for shame from having been found guilty of theft, from fear of punishment, by a husband at the death of his wife, by a wife at the death of her husband, or by both at the death of their children - are not uncommon.....The love of life is not among the New Zealanders' strongest feelings," wrote Ernst Dieffenbach in his book, *Travels in New Zealand.* [13]

In the words of Judge F.E. Maning, "No more marked alteration in the habits of the natives has taken place than in the great decrease in cases of suicide. In the first years of my residence in the country [the early 1830s] it was of almost daily occurrence. When a man died it was almost a matter of course that his wife, or wives, hung themselves. When the wife died, the man very commonly shot himself. I have known young men, often on the most trifling affront or vexation, shoot themselves; and I was acquainted with a man who, having been for two days plagued with the toothache, cut his throat with a very blunt razor without a handle; which certainly was a radical cure.

I do not believe that one case of suicide occurs now, for twenty when I first came into the country.....I think the reason suicide has become so comparatively unfrequent is that the minds of the natives are now filled and agitated by a flood of new ideas, new wants and ambitions, which they knew not formerly, and which prevents them from one single loss or disappointment, feeling as if there was nothing more to live for." [14]

The frequency of suicide was also mentioned by John Nicholas who accompanied Samuel Marsden to New Zealand in 1814-5. "The principal causes that retard the increase of population in New Zealand are the following: the degraded state in which the women are held; the universal practice of polygamy among the higher classes; preposterous superstitions; **the frequency of suicides;** and the people not being united under one head but divided into small, independent tribes under their respective chiefs, whose jealousy of each other involves them in perpetual hostility." [15]

The need for superstition as a means of social control ended with the introduction to New Zealand for the first time of a system of law and order that came with British sovereignty. A Christian sense of right and wrong as preached by the missionaries together with an overall enforceable authority in the form of the colonial government rendered superstition unnecessary and so the natives were freed from all sorts of unreal fears and mental anguish often leading to suicide that the *tohungas* and chiefs had tormented them with since time immemorial. As Chief Karaitiana told the Kohimarama Conference in 1860, "Formerly, in the days of my childhood, I asked my fathers about their customs. They replied, 'They are only the false sayings of your ancestors'." [16]

CHAPTER 9

SLAVERY

"Being a slave, it was his duty to do anything he was ordered to."

Te Rou or The Maori at Home, John White. [1]

❝Slavery is a socio-economic institution, in which some human individuals, called slaves, become the property of others, called masters or owners.....Deprived of any human rights, slaves are the unconditional possession of their owners: mere chattels, having no right to leave, refuse work or receive compensation for their labour. The position of slaves in society in many respects is akin to that of domesticated animals. Just as cows, horses and other beasts of burden are trained and utilised for economic advantage, such as for pulling carts or ploughing fields - slaves are exploited for the benefit, comfort and economic well-being of the owner....Slavery, in essence, is the exploitation of the weak by the strong," wrote M.A. Khan in his informative book, *Jihad; Blood and Slavery - From Muhammad to ISIS.* [2] Slavery, which used to be widespread, still exists to-day in certain Islamic countries such as Saudi Arabia, Sudan, Mauretania and, of course, those parts of the Middle East controlled by Islamic State (ISIS).

Needless to say, slavery was an integral part of Maori society prior to colonisation. However, although on the lowest rung of the social ladder, the condition of slaves in New Zealand was not unduly or unnecessarily cruel. Some had been taken from the losing side in a battle and, as former warriors, they were regarded by some of their captor tribes with a certain amount of respect. Conditions varied from tribe to tribe.

When a tribe was about to make an attack on another or was about to be attacked, the male slave was expected to fight for the tribe that had enslaved him. Since fighting was in the blood such slaves were often keen to do so. "The able-bodied slaves are always expected to fight in the quarrels of their masters; to do which they are nothing loth." During the tribal discussion before a battle, slaves were sometimes allowed to speak and give their views. [3]

Maori slaves were not bound in chains or anything like that; how could they be when there was no metal prior to contact with European ships after 1769? In the words of Rev. J. Buller, "It was on the whole a mild regime. The slaves generally became an integral part of the tribe to which they belonged. If noted for skill or valour, a slave could rise to distinction, and a woman of high rank would not object to him for a husband; but he was ever open to the reproach of slavery and, in the case of offence, would be taunted even by his own children.

It was the fate of the slave that he could claim no status. He was the absolute property of his owner; just as his dog or his pig. His life was valued at no higher rate; and at his death the honour of a ceremonial was denied him. In the old times, when a chief died, his slaves were killed, that they might attend his spirit to the Reinga [Cape Reinga]; and at any time, by the bidding of his caprice, a chief could take the life of a slave, and did so, oftentimes, in the most wanton manner. No one would condescend to notice it. 'He can do what he likes with his own' would be the only remark." [4]

In the words of Edward Jerningham Wakefield, "The condition of a New Zealand slave is indeed rarely very painful or oppressed.....To be sure, they hold their life at the mercy of their lord, and obey his orders under penalty of death; but they rarely do harder work than the other members of the tribe, and are not separated from the society and conversation of their masters, unless the latter be of remarkably tyrannical or avaricious disposition...[Te] Rauparaha wantonly killed one of his slaves who brought him tribute at the Mana feast in 1839 in order to serve a dainty dish to his Ngati Raukawa allies. Rangihaeata [nephew of Te Rauparaha] once took a young slave-child by the heels and dashed its brains out against a post in Otaki *pa* for breaking his pipe while lighting it. A chief at Taupo in the interior threw his slave into one of the boiling ponds there for stealing a few potatoes." [5]

In many cases slaves were referred to by European eye-witnesses in the expression "women, boys and slaves". For example, John White wrote in his book, *Te Rou or The Maori at Home*, of an early morning scene in a *pa*: "The slaves and women were all life and bustle, lighting the fires at the *hangis* with which to cook the morning meal". [6]

Some slaves had an easier ride than others. In the same book White quoted a slave, Pipo, speaking of his earlier life before he had been captured in battle. "My father had taken a slave at Taupo and, as he was younger than myself, he gave him to me to cook my fern-root, clean my fish, and go with me to catch birds. This boy slept near me." [7]

Nevertheless, a slave was an item of trade. Writing of a certain Tapapa, Rev. Williams stated, "He was originally a chief of some note at Taranaki but, during the incursions of Waikato in that quarter, he was taken prisoner with his wife and daughter. He had been brought, with many other Taranaki slaves, from Waikato to be sold to Ngapuhi for muskets and powder. Not being disposed of at the Bay of Islands, their master had intended to carry them to Hokianga and sell them there." [8]

However, where the New Zealand slave differed from slaves elsewhere was that, at any time, he could be used as a food item - either if his captor tribe ran short of food or for other reasons. In fact a slave was doubly at risk since women were not allowed to partake of the flesh of defeated warriors and so, were they cannibalistically inclined, it was only a slave that could satisfy their disgusting craving.

In the words of John White, "The young girl joined the group laughing and saying, as she put her basket down beside the other three, 'Let me eat of yours, and you can eat of that fish'.

'No,' answered her brother, one of the young men;'"you cannot eat man's flesh: you are a woman.'

'How learned you are!' she answered. 'I am older than you are.' While saying this she snatched a joint from one of the young men and, tearing a large mouthful from it, she continued: 'You may tell lies to stupid girls. I know the flesh of men killed in war is sacred and cannot be eaten by women; but Koko was not 'a fish of Tu' [a warrior], as the proverb says. I can eat of it; and let me see the hand that will try to take this arm from me.' And, while holding the ends of the limb, she tore off the flesh by mouthfuls, leaving the fish to the young men." [9]

In their book, *The Early History of New Zealand*, Sherrin and Wallace wrote, "Mr. Earle also tells us how 'on the night of his arrival at Hokianga in the *Governor Macquarie*, a chief set one of his slaves to watch the kumara grounds in order to prevent the hogs committing havoc therein. The lad, delighted with the novelty of the vessel and more intent on seeing her coming to anchor than watching the pigs, suffered them to stray where they should not. His master, arriving when the hogs were thus trespassing, killed the boy with a blow of his tomahawk, ordered a fire to be made, and the lad's body was forthwith roasted and eaten.'

'In June, 1831 (Polack writes) a Hokianga chief [the names of the persons and their descendants being well-known, are omitted] went shooting, and previous to his leaving his village desired a female slave to prepare some sweet potatoes against his return. She did as she was told but the chief was so long absent that the food got cold, and she ate them.

On his return he demanded the meal he had ordered but was told how it had been appropriated; he then called the hapless woman to him and, without speaking a word, dispatched her with a blow on the forehead with a tomahawk. He had been for some time cohabiting with her. He sent for his friends - the body was in the meantime dressed, cooked and on their arrival eaten; and to use the expression of a chief who partook of the feast....not a bone was left unmasticated.'

Another act of similar wanton nature is narrated by the same writer [Polack[as occurring at Waihou, a river some few miles distant from the mouth of the Hokianga. 'A European named Anscow proceeded down that river in a boat, accompanied by a crew of natives; he carried with him the usual trade, such as blankets, powder and tomahawks, to purchase flax or hogs. He arrived about sunset at a village called Whakarapa and, as the tide had ceased to flow, put up there for the night. He was received hospitably and was promised a quantity of hogs early in the ensuing morning. Provisions were cooked for him and his attendants.

Anscow had not been long seated when an interesting slave girl arrived, apparently about fifteen years of age, and remarkably handsome. Her approach was no sooner discovered than an old decrepit chief woman hobbled forth from her hut and made use of the most vehement language to the girl who, it appeared, had absented herself without leave for two days.

After the old crone had vented forth her objurgations, which she was unable to continue through exhaustion, she turned to a ferocious looking fellow who was standing by her, and desired him to kill the girl immediately. The ruffian did not wait for a repetition of the request but ran to the boat and, seizing one of the tomahawks which had been brought for barter, he struck the miserable girl a blow on the forehead with the implement that cleft her head in twain. This was the work of an instant, before Anscow could interfere and purchase her, which he could have done for a musket.

The body was then decollated, opened, and the entrails washed and placed in a basket; the limbs cut in pieces at the different joints, attended with circumstances at once horribly disgusting and obscene. The head was thrown to the children as a plaything, and these little miscreants rolled it to and fro like a ball, thrusting small sticks up the nose, in the mouth, ears, etc. and latterly scooped out the eyes. The remains, in several pieces, were then put into baskets and taken to the river to be cleansed by being mangled on the ground. The ovens were heated, some vegetables scraped, and the whole was cooked. A large party partook of the body." [10]

Children seemed keen to get in on the act; after all, it was only a slave. In the words of John White in *Te Rou or The Maori at Home*, "Some of the older boys had severed the old slave's head from the body, and it had been taken possession of by one of the girls, the blood trickling down her arm and bespattering the small mat which was tied round her waist. With the other hand she held the snow-white beard, by which she opened and shut the mouth, making the teeth gnash and snap, at the same time uttering a wild yell. While doing this she rushed here and there amongst the little children, to the horror of some and the amusement of others. In one of her wild flights she put the head up to the face of a slave who was passing, and made it gnash at him." [11]

These horrid, centuries old practices were ended by the arrival of Europeans, and the missionaries in particular. As Rev. Buller wrote in his book, *Forty Years in New Zealand,* "Among the fruits of Christianity was the abolition of slavery. The chiefs voluntarily made a great sacrifice in permitting their slaves, that chose to do so, to return to their ancestral homes. Most of the natives of Taranaki who in later years were in arms against the colonial Government were of this class. The demoralising effects of abject servitude remained with them. But there were others who preferred to continue with their masters, and their tribes, with which they had become incorporated." [12]

For those slaves who had not been released by 1840 the Treaty of Waitangi did the deed for them, its Article Third giving the rights of British subjects to all the people of New Zealand, including the slaves. Since slavery had recently been outlawed throughout the British Empire these hitherto unfree people attained their liberty. Not only free in their movements and choice of employment but also free of the previously ever present fear of being killed and eaten by their captors.

CHAPTER 10

WOMEN

> *"The females....are burdened with all the heavy work; they have to cultivate the fields, to carry from their distant plantations wood and provisions, and to bear heavy loads during their travelling excursions. The women generally do the whole of the planting and the gathering in of the crops....It is no uncommon thing to observe her carrying upwards of a hundred weight on her back, up a steep hill, for the men will not degrade themselves by carrying provisions, particularly on their backs.....[Women] have the appearance of being aged, when about twenty-five to thirty - and after about thirty-five they become truly ugly."*
>
> Sydney Herald, 3rd July, 1837. "Sketches in New Zealand"

❝To despise and to degrade the female sex is the characteristic of the savage state in every part of the globe. Man, proud of excelling in strength and in courage, the chief marks of pre-eminence among rude people, treats women as an inferior, with disdain." [1]

"It is only in states where rudeness and barbarism are found to exist that those beings, who were designed by nature to be the solace of man in his progress through life, are made wretched slaves to his presumptuous tyranny", wrote John Nicholas after observing the natives of New Zealand in 1814 and 1815. "Thus it happens in New Zealand, where woman is born only to labour incessantly for her taskmaster; and though, while health remains, she exerts the whole of it in his service, yet the period soon arrives when hardships and privations exhaust her frame and she becomes incapable of further drudgery.

The term of pro-creation is also short from the same cause; and most of the women of this country cease at an early age to bring forth children. But let it not be supposed from these remarks that the New

Zealanders treat their women with wanton cruelty, while they oblige them to perpetual toil. It is far otherwise and they conceive [that] they are only claiming the right they are entitled to as superior beings in making them, as an inferior species, work instead of themselves..... Most savage tribes, I rather think, are unconscious of any severity towards their women in thus consigning them to toilsome servitude; and it is fortunate for the latter that they never consider it an injustice or degradation." [2]

"The women, though doomed to a state of degraded and toilsome servitude, are under no restraint in the presence of the chiefs; and mingling in their festivities during the hours of relaxation, they seem for the time to forget their inferiority." [3]

When the tribe was preparing for war the women were not idle. "Like a flash of lightning they were all on their feet, dancing and putting out their tongues at the warriors, the youngest of the women going close up to them and making the most devilish faces and contortions of body they could, the other women dancing like mad beings." [4]

Some women would accompany a war party; these could be every bit as bloodthirsty as the fighting men. "It is customary for a few women to accompany a war expedition as attendants, their duty being twofold: to help the slaves in cooking, and to eat the *kai popoa* (sacred food) for the goddesses of war. Most of them had lost all the gentle characteristics of their sex and had almost become fiends. They had never been mothers, hence the feelings which prompted them; and if it ever occurred that the men seemed inclined to show mercy, they aroused them to fury and deeds of cruelty by language which such women alone could use. Their power was like that of setting expiring embers again into a blaze.

In all cases they headed the *whakatoa-moa* dance, a dance of insult, during which they rehearsed all the unavenged wrongs of the tribe. They were the very incarnation of revenge and wielded the power of stirring up the most fiendish feelings of the human heart, and prompting to deeds which the deadliest enemy of man might blush to witness". [5]

Sometimes these feisty females would engage in prize fights. A widow "jumped up and was in the act of springing to the rescue of her cap when the blighted one caught hold of her, and the two struggled, screamed and tore each other.....On came the bare footed crowd of men, women, boys, girls and little children. The noise was at its height. The two struggling women in their fury had torn nearly all the covering from each other and were now rolling and tumbling, now up, now down, occasionally coming in contact with a burning ember, the pain caused by which kept up their fury, as each thought the other had either bitten or pinched her..... The boys and girls, in the wild spirit of youth, enjoyed the sight of the two struggling women, who had become exhausted and could scarcely hold each other." [6]

The savagery of the tribeswomen was also on display in the camps where the men were preparing for battle. "The women were busy heating the *hangis* for the evening meal of fish, and while doing so discussed the probable result of the coming battle with as little feeling as though they were talking of catching a few fish. Said an old wrinkled woman to some young ones who were sitting quiet, looking at the children having their war-dance, while she bent down and looked into their faces, 'I am glad we are so numerous for our people are sure to gain the battle and I shall get some flesh for my poor pup. It really has had nothing but fern-root and sow-thistle for some time'. Then, standing up erect, she added in a low voice, 'Yes, and I must remember to dry some flesh so that it will keep for some time. I and my dog can eat it dried well enough'." [7]

Another burden that women had to bear was polygamy. "Polygamy is universal among these islanders, and the number of wives varies in proportion to the circumstances of the individual, there being, however, a head wife who is treated with particular respect and holds an ascendancy over the husband." [8]

"The higher orders form an interested conjunction with several women, none of whom, except her who is emphatically termed the head wife, can be said to experience any of the enjoyments of matrimony, living with their nominal husbands in the degraded state I have described and as handmaids to the favoured spouse. Though obliged, when once married, to submit for life to conjugal restraints (death, under certain circumstances, being the sure consequence of any dereliction) still, as they are generally neglected for the head wife, the intercourse between them and the men who claim their fidelity is unfrequent, which of course must be unfavourable to the propagation of the human species," wrote John Nicholas. [9]

This was also noted by Rev. William Williams. "It was clear that the plurality of wives among the natives was a great injustice. The proportion of the sexes has been found to be painfully unequal. Throughout the country there are about four males to three females. A chief was allowed to take as many wives as he pleased but many a poor one had none." [10]

It wasn't all one way as John White wrote of a woman who had been the wife of six husbands. "Her first husband was cooked and eaten, having fallen while attacking his enemies. Her restlessness would not allow her to cry long over the eaten one and she determined to marry a young man not half her age. By dint of following him and making love to him in her active way, she soon succeeded and he became her second husband." [11]

However, while picking some fruit up a tree he fell down on to some rocks and died. "She gave him but one look and rushed to the settlement and told what had befallen him who had been her husband but for three moons, and she sat down and cried the whole day long. The young men brought the mangled corpse to her hut and the next day a party, who had come to lament over him, took the body to their *pa* to bury him. The chief of this party had six wives and, wishing to have seven, he took the weeping widow at her request into his affections.

She had again been a wife for three moons when a general quarrel took place among the seven wives, of which she was the cause. In the midst of the noise and chatter, crying and scolding, the husband heard again and again his last espoused wife make comparisons between himself and her two former husbands; and not daring to avenge himself upon her, because of her rank and for fear that a war party of her relatives would come and kill some of his people and plunder him if he beat her, he had but one alternative and that was to withdraw directly from the noise his wives made and hang himself. This he achieved on a tree not far from the settlement. Three of his wives followed his example from sorrow but the other four married again

The next man who called this active woman his wife was choked by a fish-bone while, in a furious passion, she was scolding him. Her fifth husband hung himself because she thought he was delicate and consumptive.....Her last husband actually died in a house where she could talk to him during his illness." [12]

In the words of Rev. J. Buller, "Polygamy was common.....Usually one wife would be entitled to take rank as such, and the rest sustained the position of slaves. A chief's wealth was reckoned according to the number of his women. My old friend, Te Tirarau, had twelve wives but only one was treated with the respect due to that relation." [13]

Women were not really free in choosing a spouse. In the words of Rev. Buller, "Betrothal took place in infancy or childhood and rested on tribal considerations. Sometimes a young girl was made *tapu* for some grey-headed old chief. This was productive of much misery. As the bride-elect came to years of discretion she might have a strong dislike for her affianced or a decided preference for some other one. In such a case she would either hang herself or elope with her lover. Then arose an alarm, and a pursuit.

When the fugitives were overtaken, a struggle would follow between the friends on both sides. The strongest would carry off their victim and it was well for the poor girl if she had no joint dislocated or limb broken during the rough pulling and hauling.

If not betrothed in childhood, a marriage between two young persons was not an easy thing. Every one of her relations had a say in it; they had little of sentiment about it. Before the relatives could agree, the young couple sometimes ran off to the woods and hid themselves; and, after time had softened anger, their act would be condoned." [14]

Some husbands were brutal to their wives and could largely get away with it. In the words of F. E. Maning, writing of a high-ranking scoundrel, "I must, however, protest against the misdeeds of a few ruffians - human wolves - being charged against the whole of their countrymen. At the time I am speaking of, the only restraint on such people was the fear of retaliation, and the consequence was that often a dare-devil savage would run a long career of murder, robbery and outrage before meeting with a check, simply from the terror he inspired and the 'luck' which often accompanies outrageous daring. At a time, however, and in a country like New Zealand where every man was a fighting man or nothing, these desperadoes sooner or later came to grief, being at last invariably shot or run through the body by some sturdy freeholder, whose rights they had invaded." [15]

"He had killed several men in fair fight and had also - as was well known - committed two most diabolical murders, one of which was on his own wife, a fine young woman whose brains he blew out at half a second's notice for no further provocation than this: - he was sitting in the verandah of his house and told her to bring him a light for his pipe. She, being occupied in domestic affairs, said, 'Can't you fetch it yourself? I am going for water.'

She had the calibash in her hand and their infant child on her back. He snatched up his gun and instantly shot her dead on the spot; and I heard him afterwards describing quite coolly the comical way in which her brains had been knocked out by the shot with which the gun was loaded." [16]

As late as 1849, when *HMS Acheron* was surveying the coast of New Zealand so as to make it safer for shipping, a party from the ship went on an inland trip from Lyttelton during which they stopped at a native village and conversed with a chief called Charley, who showed them his new wife, a girl of sixteen. This was his second wife. In the words of Mr. Hansard, the diarist for the *Acheron*, "The former rib had played him false so, quoth he, 'I broke her head and her mother's head, and turned them out; and this one, if she deceives me, I'll break her head too'." [17]

Like the Hindu custom of suttee, the women were expected to kill themselves when their husband died. As an old chief lay dying he gave his last testament with the words, "I give my *mere* to my *pakeha*, my two old wives will hang themselves (here a howl of assent from the two old women in the rear rank)." [18]

"Men keep their youthful looks longer than women," wrote John White. [19] Not surprising since the women and slaves did all the hard physical work while their male kin lounged around in the sun and were only really useful as warriors.

It was the coming of colonisation which rescued women from their degraded state and so for the first time in the history of Maoridom the women attained the dignity and rights that were due to them as human beings. In fact, within a few decades (1893) Maori women would be among the rest of New Zealand females who became the first in the world to gain a parliamentary vote at national elections. From inequality to equality. From inferior status and fear to the security of living under British rule. The only occasions when part-Maori women are made to feel inferior to-day are when they attend some tribal function on a marae or elsewhere and are made to sit in the back seats while the men of the tribe hog all the front chairs in most ungentlemanly fashion.

A sailing ship in sight of Mount Egmont, bringing settlers from England to a new life in New Zealand. See pages 109-14.

Scene at the mouth of the Turanganui River, Gisborne, at the time of Captain Cook's landing there on 8th October, 1769. The fortifications on both sides of the river indicate the insecurity due to tribal warfare. Below is the same spot after colonisation, showing both security and prosperity.

By 1903, when this picture was taken, the Auckland waterfront reflected the tremendous progress of the city and hinterland - a far cry from the pre-1840 period when the Auckland isthmus was deserted because no tribe felt secure enough to live there. See page 80-1.

Cows first came to New Zealand on board the Active with Rev. Samuel Marsden in 1814. See page 12.

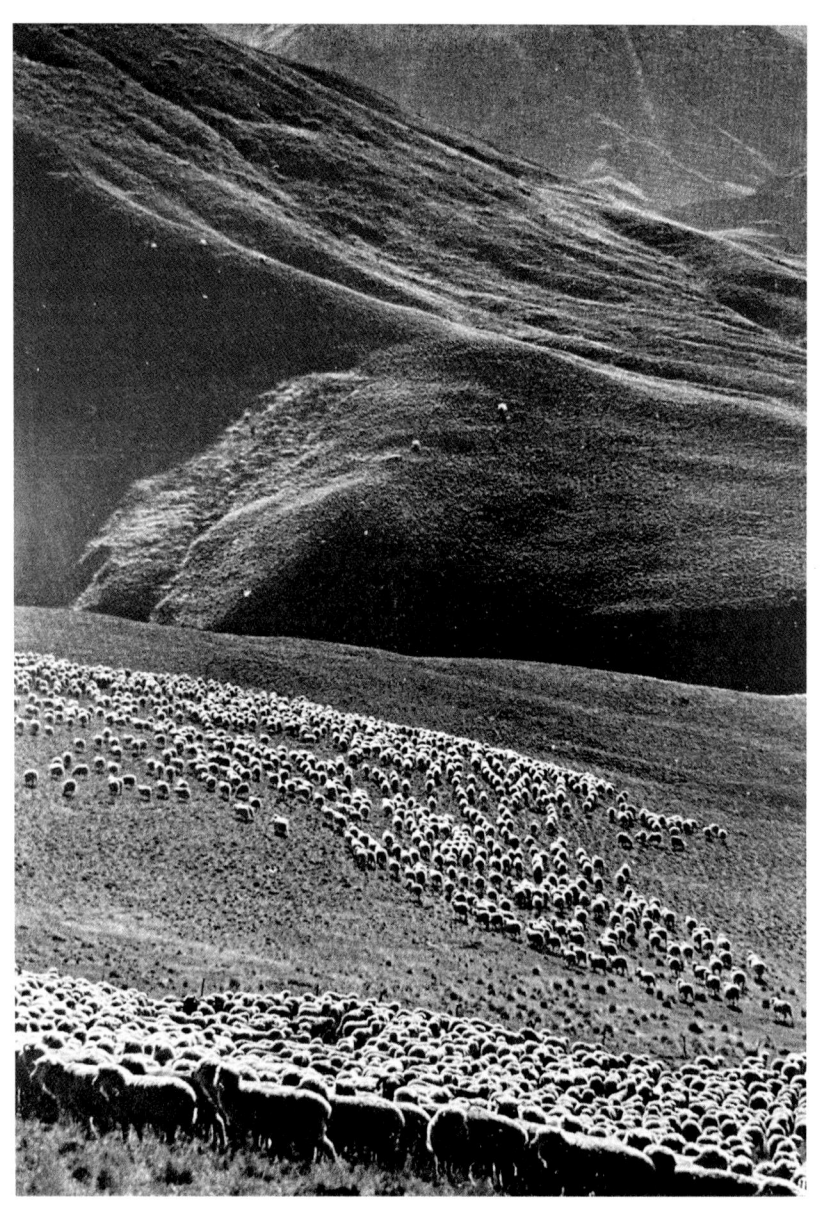

The European settlers brought with them horses, cows, goats, pigs and sheep. After the kauri was exhausted, wool and meat became the backbone of the economy.

CHAPTER 11

CHILDREN

"Children were subject to no restraint as they grew up". [1]

There was rejoicing at the birth of a child, particularly if of great rank in the tribe". [2] However, like the cruel practice of binding girls' feet in China to make them small so that old men could suck them, the early days for a native child in New Zealand could be perilous and painful.

"The infant's nose was flattened; the knee joints were rubbed down in order to reduce the inner part and make them handsome. To do this the nurse placed the child, with its face downwards, on her lap and the legs and knees were rubbed down, with much squeezing of the inner knee. This process was repeated daily, for many weeks. Female children had the first joint of the thumb bent outwards [so] that they might be the better able in after-life to scrape, weave and plait the flax leaf. While very young the lobes of the ears were pierced with a sharp-pointed stone (obsidian) for the sake of wearing ornaments, of sharks' teeth, bird skins or greenstone". [3]

The "might is right" concept was drummed into children at an early age, making them savage before adulthood. "Some of the children were running here and there in savage glee, with spears in their hands; while here and there groups of them were sitting listening to a child orator and warrior, who entranced his listeners with a wild account of the doings of his ancestors; while others of them might be seen dancing the war-dance with fiendish glee." [4]

Of an eleven year old boy, Moe, John White wrote in *Te Rou; or the Maori at Home*, "Moe....went not so much in obedience to his mother's command as because it suited his inclination. Children of his age, about eleven summers old, hold it as an undisputed point that they are their own masters and can do whatever they please, unless thwarted by someone stronger than themselves.

Kaikai was expending the strength of his arm, tongue and voice to the great amusement of a lot of men, women, boys and girls. He had made a large circular fire, about two strides wide; around this he placed, on sticks about a yard long and stuck around the fire, the limbs of Koko. A leg was stuck with the foot in the air, the stick having stuck in at the thigh end, and pushed up to the knee; an arm came next, the stick having been stuck right up to the elbow; one side of the ribs was put between the split end of a stick, the ends being tied together to keep the ribs from falling out.

As the heat acted upon the limbs Kaikai said, 'Now, children, old Koko will show you how to use your arms in the *kauikaui [haka]*. Look, look how that arm twists! See, the old man is about to walk! Look, his thigh quivers! There', he said as one of the legs fell down, 'he will kick you if you do not stand farther off.' At the same time swinging the limb round, which was now hot, he struck a number of the children with it, who ran away screaming and laughing, each rubbing that part of their body where the cooked limb had hit them." [5]

At the tender age of eleven Moe was already a cannibal. Speaking to an older man during such a feast, Moe said of the flesh, "It is good. You would like it if you tried some."

"Would you like to eat me?" asked the old man.

"O no!" answered Moe.

"Then why do you eat Koko?" asked the old man. "He was kind to you."

"O, Kai told me he could not feel me chewing him now that he is cooked," answered Moe, "and, as his flesh would rot and do no good but breed blow-flies, there is no harm in eating him. And I shall eat our enemies when I am a man. I can learn to be brave now that I am little".

The old man asked, "How would you like to eat the flesh of a little boy as big as you are?"

"Why do such children allow themselves to be killed?" answered Moe. "If they cannot keep out of the way when our people go to fight, that is their own fault for not keeping out of the way." [6]

The kicking around the *pa* of severed heads and other limbs seems to have been an early form of football for the children of the tribes. "Immediately there was a rush to get possession of the head, and the children rolled and tumbled over each other. It was this that had caused the little boy to laugh. One of the boys had gained possession of an arm, and placed it on the fire to roast the flesh near the shoulder. This act had been seen by a slave who, because of his great muscular strength, had with impunity done many things which men in his position did not ordinarily dare to do.

He stepped up behind the boy (who was in the act of putting the cooked flesh to his mouth), and suddenly jerked it out of his hand; at the same time the boy fell on his back. The slave tore off a few mouthfuls and threw the arm down again, and ran away to escape an attack from the enraged lad and his associates.

As soon as the boy regained his legs he seized the arm and, with a spiteful yell, threw it after the slave. The aim not being good, it went rolling and tumbling in the air, and fell near to a wrinkled, decrepit, half-blind old woman, who had just before been begging for a limb. Taking this as one thrown to her, she snatched it up and put it under her mat, her face at the same time lighting up with a smile of supreme delight." [7]

This behaviour on the part of children was viewed with approval by their elders. "You remember we cooked and ate them, and made their bones into fishing hooks; the children played with their heads, sticking them on sticks and making speeches to them, then holding a *hahunga* over them, as children will do. All this delighted us for we thought how brave our children would be." [8]

The son of a noted *tohunga*, who later converted to Christianity, told the missionary, Mr. Davis, "Before I was yet born my father devoted me to the powers of darkness. As soon as I was able to struggle for my mother's breast I was often teased by my father and kept from it in order that angry passions might be deeply rooted in me. The stronger I grew, the more I was teased by my father, and the harder I had to fight for nourishment. All this was done before I was old enough to notice the plants which are produced by the earth.

When I could run about the work of preparation went on more rigidly, and my father kept me without food that I might learn to thieve, not forgetting, at the same time, to stir up the spirit of anger and revenge which he had so assiduously endeavoured to implant in my breast. My father then taught me how to bewitch and destroy people at my pleasure; and he told me that, to be a great man, I must be a bold murderer, a desperate and expert thief, and able to do all kinds of wickedness effectually.

I recollect while I was a child my father went to kill pigs. I tried to get a portion for myself but my father beat me away because I had not been active in killing them. When the tribe went to war and I was able to go with them, I endeavoured to fulfil my father's wishes by committing acts of violence; and, when I succeeded in catching slaves for myself, my father was pleased and said, 'Now I will feed you because you deserve it; now you shall not be in want of good things'." [9]

Such were the upbringings of children in what Rev. William Williams called "that benighted land". [10] They were lifted out of this darkness and horror by first the missionaries, who preached the love of Christ, and then after 1840 by the imposition of British law, which outlawed such conduct. But the mental damage of this brutalising behaviour would not vanish immediately.

The uncertain survivalist lifestyle produced a "maximum aggressive" trait in the victors and/or a "borderline personality condition" and heightened state of fear among those awaiting their fate, both contributing to serious psychological harm.

It is fashionable in the twenty-first century for some defence barristers, social workers and academics to blame "colonisation" for the high rate of offending by part-Maoris, especially in relation to crimes of violence. The truth, however, is the exact opposite. If there is mental damage that lasts down the generations, it is because of the barbaric and brutalising nature of Maori society over the centuries - conditions that they were mercifully rescued from by "colonisation" in the form of the missionaries, a settled law across the land and the Queen's Peace, which was broken only by the decisions of Hone Heke in the 1840s and the Kingites in the 1860s to take up arms against the lawful authority.

CHAPTER 12

INFANTICIDE

Before the introduction of English law in 1840 the life of a female Maori baby was not by any means secure. "The practice of infanticide and, in particular of female infanticide, is of particular importance to the story of the Maori as this had a significant impact on population dynamics, continuing until the second half of the nineteenth century......it was prevalent and often observed," wrote John Robinson. [1]

"Infanticide was frequent and in many cases as the result of jealousy. A male child was seldom sacrificed because of his future value as a warrior," wrote Rev. J. Buller. [2]

"Infanticide is very common, particularly among the women of the Bay of Islands district, where they are frequently chapu (enceinte) by Europeans but, as the birth and necessary attendance for many months on a young child would materially injure their pecuniary interests in not being able to proceed as usual on board of the whalers, and thereby assist their fathers or brothers with the presents they obtain by a liberal distribution of their favours, the poor young one but seldom sees the light, abortion being generally produced within the first month or two of pregnancy....A woman who has been taken a prisoner, and was chapu at the time, will generally (if the party who captures her takes her as unto himself as a wife, and the affection on her side is returned) kill the child the moment it is born, and this is considered as a great proof of affection towards her new husband, and may very likely ensure her kinder treatment." [3]

And the early trader, Joel Polack: "I think the principal cause is infanticide. I have seen many women who have destroyed their children, either by abortion or, after their birth, putting them into a basket and throwing them into the sea, after pressing the frontal bones of their heads." [4]

"Nathaniel Turner met a woman who discussed female infanticide as a matter of pleasure rather than otherwise, and referred us to some of the most respectable among them, with whom we were acquainted who had thus destroyed their own children. The usual manner of putting them to death is squeezing the nose as soon as they are born. This they call *romeo*," wrote Ormond Wilson in *From Hongi Hika to Hone Heke*. [5]

With the liaisons between Maori women and European seamen and traders, females came to be more highly valued for what a white man would pay for their company. "The illicit intercourse, it is said, between the British seamen and the unmarried females, has put an end to the most extensive system of infanticide ever known. A universal and unnatural custom among them, which was that of destroying most of their female children in infancy - the few females who were suffered to live were invariably looked down upon by all with the utmost contempt.

The difference now is most remarkable. The natives, seeing with what admiration strangers beheld their fine young women, and what handsome presents were made to them, by which their families were benefitted, feeling also that their influence was so powerful, have been latterly as anxious to cherish and protect their infant girls as they were formerly cruelly bent on destroying them," wrote the *Sydney Herald* on 29th July, 1833.

At the Bay of Islands, in the words of a "respectable correspondent" in 1837, "All chiefs are continually on board some of the numerous vessels that frequent their harbour, either to sell their produce or begging a glass of spirits, of which they are inordinately fond, but principally to see what payment they can obtain from the master and crew of the vessels by the sale, for the time being, of their daughters, sisters or female slaves.

This species of traffic is carried on to an immense extent, and not only are thousands of pounds annually given to them for this branch of commerce but the owners of vessels also suffer greatly by the bread cask being continually open to them, as well as by the waste and destruction of quantities of fresh provisions, which are daily given to their relations, principally from the captain's table, in order to ensure the continuance on board during the stay of the ship of the temporary wives of the master and officers. I should say that the natives of the Bay of Islands receive a revenue by the sale of their women and what they steal of at least, £7,000 annually." [6]

Infanticide was no less a problem when a Maori woman had a baby by a European man. In the words of the *New Zealand Gazette and Wellington Spectator* of 12th January, 1842, "In these islands there are a large number of Europeans cohabiting with native women and we have been surprised to find how few children are the result of this connection....We have been assured that the children are destroyed by the mothers, sometimes before, but most frequently after birth. Several persons have assured us that this is the case and a white man at Waikanae told us that he knew a native woman who had smothered five of her offspring, the father of whom was a white man. We were induced to ask the cause of this most unnatural of acts.

Though the disregard of life among savages is notorious our observations have led us to believe the native women to be devotedly affectionate mothers. We have been assured that the reason for these women doing such violence to their feelings is the fear of being deserted. They have no guarantee that the men with whom they are cohabiting will continue in the place for 24 hours. When abandoned, they return to their tribe.....

When living with their relations, if they introduce these half-castes, they are perpetually jeered and are the unceasing theme of native sarcasm; they never tire of the amusement they derive from teasing these unfortunate women about the father of their child having abandoned them to the tender mercies of their tribe."

The brutality of Maori society towards both unborn and born babies was ended with the introduction of British law in 1840. However, as might be expected, infanticide did not suddenly end with the Treaty of Waitangi; it continued in some Maori communities at a diminishing rate until the end of the nineteenth century. The other method of getting rid of a baby - murder by abortion - was legalised in the 21st century when the cruel and heartless government of Jacinda Ardern cheerfully made it legal, thus taking New Zealand on a big step backwards into its dark and brutal past.

CHAPTER 13

TRIBAL WARFARE

"Those were the days when the fight, the feast and the funeral were everyday occurrences".
Evening Post, Wellington, 10 October, 1900.

"The barbarous feuds that disfigured this beautiful land".
Dr. Hocken, historian of early New Zealand. [1]

❝War was a passion with the Maoris. Every one was trained to it from his childhood. Even the women were active auxiliaries in their martial exploits. A people so revengeful in their disposition and so energetic in their character never wanted a pretext for fighting. But the most frequent casus belli were either land or woman.... Vindictive purposes were handed down from father to son through generations. The latter never thought he had done his duty until he had redeemed the honour and fulfilled the dying wishes of his sire or grandsire. Arrears of such reckoning were always on hand and, as anyone related to the offending party, directly or remotely, was a fair prey for the 'avenger of blood', no tribe could tell when the storm of war might burst upon it, even from those who were living in peace. Hence their continual and mutual distrust," wrote Rev. J. Buller in his *Forty Years in New Zealand.* [2]

"The requirements of *utu* and the possibility of action against some third party with no connection to the initial cause (*take*) to assuage the angry feelings of the heart would often multiply the disputes and give reason for further fighting," wrote John Robinson in his book,

Unrestrained Slaughter.[3] This made for a heady and terrible mix and, even before the use of the musket, the constant inter-tribal fighting was ruining Maori society.

"The perpetual hostility, in which these poor savages, who have made every village a fort, must necessarily live, will account for there being so little of their land in a state of cultivation; and as mischiefs very often reciprocally produce each other, it may perhaps appear that there being so little land in cultivation will account for their living in perpetual hostility", wrote Captain Cook when he first visited New Zealand in 1769.[4]

The fighting was invariably vicious. "Every cruelty was inflicted on the vanquished. Their blood was quaffed while warm; their heads preserved, their bodies cooked. Before they had firearms their conflicts were hand-to-hand....When the victorious army returned with the trophies of conquest, they were greeted by the women with hideous noises, grimaces and contortions. Those of them who had lost husbands or brothers or sons would wreak their vengeance on the wretched captives...The heads of the fallen foes were preserved; the brain, the tongue, the eyes were scooped out and the cavities filled up with fern or flax, then boiled in water till the thick skin was easily peeled off," wrote Buller.[5]

One of the bloodiest battles was fought in 1831 at Pukerangiora in Taranaki when Waikato attacked Te Atiawa. "Te Wherowhero's warriors ran them down....It is said that at least 200 [Te Atiawa] escapees died immediately, with Te Wherowhero killing 150 single-handedly with blows to the head. It was only when his arm grew tired and swollen that he was forced to stop.....The scene that followed was terrible, with huge numbers of the dead gutted and spit-roasted over fires. Some Waikato warriors indulged in a feast of such gluttony that they died. In desperation women threw their children off the cliff into the Waitara River and jumped in after them rather than have them captured alive. It is thought that as many as 1,200 Te Atiawa people lost their lives at Pukerangiora."[6]

Women were not spared. "After Hongi was wounded another *pa* was taken where a great number of the natives had sought refuge, and men, women and children were all massacred without any regard to age or sex. Hongi gave orders that no one should be spared except the slaves, who were to be incorporated into his tribe." [7]

"Ngai Tahu went back to Port Underwood where they killed several women (Maori wives of whalers), drove the whalers off and destroyed their homes and stock of whale oil." [8]

In the Bay of Plenty "The premises of Mr. Tapsell, a flax trader, were burnt to the ground and all his property either destroyed or carried away. So completely indeed was the place ransacked that the natives dug up the body of Mr. Tapsell's child, which had been deeply buried in his garden, in the hope of finding treasure in the coffin." [9]

"Many of the captured were kept as slaves and held like cattle on the hoof, to be killed and eaten later".[10] In the summer of 1831-2 Te Rauparaha, probably the most vicious cannibal of them all, led his Ngati Toa against the Ngai Tahu fort at Kaiapoi. Upon capture of the *pa*, Rauparaha devoured some of the prisoners himself, "tearing open the living mother and holding the half-formed embryo upon a pointed stick in the flames to be afterwards devoured." [11]

With the coming of the musket, especially after Hongi Hika's visit to England where gullible people showered this "noble savage" with gifts, which he sold for muskets in Sydney on his way home, the killing reached new heights. In fact, there were approximately 3,000 battles and raids fought among the tribes between 1807 and 1845. [12]

"It was obvious that Maori society was destroying itself," wrote Dr. Robinson in *Unrestrained Slaughter; the Maori Musket Wars, 1800-1840.* [13] "Ngapuhi had been leaders in this social suicide by building up their stocks of arms and expanding the total, unlimited musket war that was wiping out entire communities." [14]

"If the chiefs were asked when their wars would be at an end, they replied 'never' because it is the custom of every tribe which loses a man not to be content without satisfaction, and nothing less than the death of one individual can atone for the death of another," wrote Rev. William Williams. [15]

"This was a time of genocide, a true holocaust; the wars had a huge impact on the Maori population. Professor Sir Peter Buck accepted the estimate of 80,000 who were killed in battle or died of causes incidental to the wars as probably correct. Surveyor-General, ethnologist, pioneer Maori-Polynesian historian and founder of the Polynesian Society, Stephenson Percy Smith, gave the same estimate when he noted that 'the missionaries, who had fairly good means of judging, estimated that the decrease in population during the first third of the nineteenth century, due to war, famine and their accompaniments, to be about 80,000 souls'.....

There was considerable social disruption as many were driven from their traditional lands into the bush, with poor food and living conditions while fertile lands were left empty - with increased mortality. Many areas were deserted." [16]

"Historian Michael King has written of the musket wars, 'If any chapter in New Zealand history has earned the label 'holocaust', it is this one.'[17] In fact, this was probably the worst holocaust in terms of proportion of lives lost that the world has ever seen, carried out by the people themselves." [18]

The figures given above by Sir Peter Buck and Stephenson Percy Smith can only be estimates as pre-colonisation Maori lacked a Statistics Department or a register of births, deaths and marriages. Professor James Rutherford, formerly professor of history at Auckland University, has given a lower estimate. After taking account of more than 600 battles fought between 1805 and 1840, he estimated the native death toll at 43,600 with a further 10,000 likely to have died as a result of "hardship during dispersals". [19]

In the words of R. D. Crosby in his book, *The Musket Wars*, "Of an estimated 100,000 - 150,000 Maori living in New Zealand at or around 1810, by 1840 probably somewhere between 50,000 and 60,000 had been killed, enslaved or forced to migrate as a result of the wars (working from estimates generated by Ian Pool and others). In the main that occurred in the short space of twenty-five years from 1815 to 1840." [20]

Sir Peter Buck's figure of 80,000 would represent around half the population being killed in these wars while Rutherford's lower estimate of deaths would represent about a third of the total estimated native population of the time.

These horrific proportions of the population killed are far greater than the two largest genocides of recent times: Cambodia and Rwanda (which latter used to be spelt on National Geographic maps as "Ruanda"). Between 1975 and 1979 an estimated 1.5 to 3 million Cambodians were killed by the Communist Khmer Rouge regime out of a total population in 1975 of 7.3 million. [21] Between April and July, 1994, some 500,000 to 662,000 people (mostly those of the Tutsi tribe) were butchered in Rwanda by the Hutu tribe out of a total population of 5.936 million. [22]

Had the tribal wars continued at their going rate, the natives would have wiped themselves out to extinction. As it was, the depopulation of their race was considerable. "The population of the North Island was thinned and scattered; and that of the Middle [South] Island destroyed, with the exception of a miserable remnant," wrote Edward Jerningham Wakefield. [23]

"The natives attribute their decrease in numbers, before the arrival of the Europeans, to war and sickness; disease possibly arising from the destruction of food and the forced neglect of cultivation caused by the constant and furious wars which devastated the country for a long period before the arrival of the Europeans; and to such an extent that the natives had at last believed a constant state of warfare to be the natural condition of life, and their sentiments, feelings and maxims became gradually formed on this belief. Nothing was so valuable or respectable as strength and courage, and to acquire property by war and plunder was more honourable and also more desirable than by labour. Cannibalism was glorious. In a word, the island was a pandemonium." [24]

The root of the problem was that there was no sovereign in New Zealand strong enough to govern the place and keep the peace and so the hundreds of tribes and sub-tribes continued in glorious anarchy and bloodshed. "During these years the tribal culture was not just dysfunctional; it was crazy, criminally insane. The consequences of those decades of killing, social disruption, destruction of crops, infanticide, fear and uncertainty was a society in shock. There was widespread desolation and devastation among tribal communities," wrote Andy Oakley in his book, *Cannons Creek to Waitangi*. [25]

From about 1820 the tribes of the Northland peninsula in particular were slowly brought around to the view that war was wasteful and destructive by the arguments of the missionaries. This, as we shall see later, was the mindset that finally persuaded them to ask for a single sovereign to govern their anarchic land and that could only be Queen Victoria, the monarch who presided over the greatest empire that the world had ever seen - one that was based on law and order as well as a high degree of personal freedom, things that were hitherto unknown to Maori society.

CHAPTER 14

CANNIBALISM

By far the most horrible aspect of traditional Maori life, from which they were rescued by the merciful introduction of Christianity and British law, was cannibalism, which is as degrading as humans can go. In fact, cannibalism was a major driving force in pre-colonisation Maori life and was often the motive for warfare.

Around 1820 a war party, consisting of former enemies, Ngapuhi and Ngati Whatua, joined forces in Northland and walked in their bare feet all the way down the west coast of the North Island to Wellington, attacking, killing and eating other tribes as they went.

Then in 1821 Ngati Whatua and Waikato tribes were joined by adventurers from Ngati Maniapoto, Ngati Maru, Ngati Raukawa and Te Arawa in an even longer march. They went from south Auckland to the east of Lake Taupo, then down the Hawkes Bay and through Wairarapa to Wellington and then up the west coast around Taranaki to Auckland.

It s perhaps understandable why tribes living near each other would go to war against each other over land or women, etc. but the most likely explanation for these massive hikes of warriors through difficult bush-clad country to kill and eat members of tribes with which they were unlikely to have had problems was their hunger for human flesh. Thousands of tribespeople were killed and eaten by these two rampaging war parties in what can probably be described as the two largest and longest cannibal feasts in human history. A giant "progress party" from one native settlement to the next.

"Abhorrent as this subject is to the common feelings of mankind.... it marks so decidedly the character of these people," wrote John Nicholas.[1] Indeed it did. When in 1830 Captain Stewart so shamefully carried Te Rauparaha and his Ngati Toa warriors from Kapiti Island to Akaroa on Banks Peninsula in his ship, the *Elizabeth*, the Ngai Tahu enemies were invited on board where they were taken prisoner by Rauparaha's warriors, who had been hiding in the hold of the ship.

"In the early hours of the next morning the *taua* went ashore..... Takapuneke *pa* and surrounding villages were savagely attacked. Two hundred men were killed and perhaps three hundred or four hundred women and children; many were also brought aboard the ships as slaves. Heaps of men were left dead ashore. Cannibal feasting continued on the journey home". [2] In fact, so much human flesh had been cooked in the *umu* ovens on the beach that they couldn't eat it all at the time and so it was placed in about a hundred flax baskets which they ate during the next few days on the voyage back to Kapiti - a type of "doggy bag". [3]

At Kapiti the Ngai Tahu chief, Te Maiharanui and one of his wives, Te Whe, "were cut open and their blood drunk, until at length Te Maiharanui was put out of his misery by a red-hot ramrod being passed through his neck." [4] This sort of thing is enough to disgust anybody with an atom of humanity in them but not apparently Christopher Finlayson, the former Treaty Minister in the National Government, who in 2012 gave $10 million of taxpayers' money to Rauparaha's tribe "in compensation for Ngati Toa's loss of its maritime empire in Cook Strait" - code for the "right" of its warriors to cross the Strait on missions of terrorism and cannibalism such as the one described here. The Waitangi Tribunal, which hardly ever turns down a tribal claim, had earlier rejected this preposterous and immoral demand but Finlayson overrode them and rewarded cannibalism. This is the same seriously twisted Minister who handed over millions of dollars of public funds to the tribe at Parihaka "for rapes committed by Crown troops" during the occupation of that troublesome place in 1881 even though there is no evidence that any rape occurred!

Captain Cook attributed the cannibalism of the New Zealanders to a lack of sufficient food but this is obviously wrong. In the words of John Nicholas, "The [North] island, besides it being abundantly supplied with the fern-root.....has also plenty of other esculent roots which are very nutritious, and a profusion of the best fish, so that a scarcity of food is a thing never known in the country." [5]

He continues, "A kind of superstitious revenge is the grand actuating principle that incites them to this horrible practice. Born in the grossest ignorance and nurtured amidst wild dissensions, they give loose to all the violence of their ungovernable passions; while superstition teaches them to believe that their revenge can reach beyond the grave, and that the future existence of their wretched victims must be totally annihilated by this unnatural destruction of their mortal remains.

With this shocking idea the children are bred up from infancy; when hearing continually of bloody achievements, and learning from the lips of their fathers the various deeds of carnage in which they have been engaged, they grow up so much habituated to these enormities that they consider them congenial with their very existence, while they form the favourite topic of their conversations and the darling theme of their poetical rhapsodies." [6]

Nicholas believed that it was "the same superstition which disposes them to respect with the most scrupulous veneration the dead bodies of their friends, acting conversely, impels them to gorge themselves upon the mangled remains of their hostile opponents." [7]

This was also the view of Rev. Buller, "Cannibalism was common.... Its origin was not due to scarcity of food or the mere liking for human flesh. Hatred and revenge are their strongest passions and, under the influence of these, they came to devour their enemies. Chiefs used to pride themselves on the fame of being great cannibals. It was the utmost degradation to which they could reduce their foes - to eat them!" [8]

It is only fair to point out that not all Maoris engaged in cannibalism; some found it revolting. "I asked Jem if he had partaken of the horrid banquet," wrote John Nicholas, "but he appeared shocked at the idea, and assured me that nothing in life could prevail upon him to taste human flesh". [9] And he wasn't the only one.

However, for the few who disliked it there were many who relished the taste. Waharoa, the cannibal chief of Matamata: "How sweet will the flesh of the Rotorua natives taste along with their new kumeras". [10] Touai, a native chief who was taken to London in 1818 and spent some time there, "confessed in his moments of nostalgia that what he most regretted in the country from which he was absent was the feast of human flesh, the feast of victory. He was weary of eating English beef. He claimed that there was a great analogy between the flesh of the pig and that of man. This last declaration he made before a sumptuously served table. The flesh of women and children was to him and his fellow-countrymen the most delicious." [11]

The feast would often take the nature of a party. "Rising, she went to a group of young men who were laughing and joking while enjoying the cooked limbs, which by this time had been torn joint from joint and were being passed from one to another of the young men, who sat in a circle round three baskets of kumeras." [12]

"When cannibalism is found common among races of men, sensual love of human flesh invariably influenced the continuance of the custom," wrote A.S. Thomson in his book, *The Story of New Zealand*. "The natives looked on human flesh as desirable and toothsome food, and scrupled not to assure Europeans that, if they were once to eat it, they would not care for pork or other meat, it was so much superior.

In the instance of two young girls who had been killed at the Bay of Islands in comparatively late years and cooked for *utu* in war, they were killed, it should be remembered, by their own sex, the women killing the girls and the men eating them. This practice was not at all a cause for comment as being unusual, but is noted to show among other facts how cannibalism brutalised both sexes." [13]

In the words of Daniel Henry Sheridan, writing of the defence of Nga-motu in 1832, "The principal part of the prisoners that day were cripples, women and children; the remainder making their escapes as well as their weak state would allow them (they had been besieged for a considerable time). A party of the enemy were employed in despatching as many as would be sufficient for the evening's meal;

their slaves getting the ovens ready, and the remainder went in search of more prey, which they found to the number of twelve hundred.

On the 23rd they commenced the slaughter of the prisoners that were taken alive. They were crammed into huts, well guarded, [with] the principal chief executioner, with a sharp tomahawk in his hand, ready to receive them. They were then called out one by one. Those that had well carved or tattooed heads had their heads cut off on a block, the body quartered and hung upon fences that were erected for the purpose. Those with indifferent heads received one blow, and were then dragged to a hole to bleed. The young children and grown up lads were cut down the belly and then roasted on sticks before the fires.....

To the gun I was stationed at they dragged a man slightly wounded in the leg, and tied him hand and foot until the battle was over. Then they loosed him and put some questions to him, which he could not answer or give them any satisfaction thereof, as he knew his doom. They then took the fatal tomahawk and put it between his teeth while another pierced his throat for a chief to drink his blood. Others at the same time were cutting his arms and legs off. They then cut off his head, quartered him and sent his heart to a chief, it being a delicious morsel and they being generally favoured with such rarities after an engagement.

In the meantime a fellow that had proved a traitor wished to come and see his wife and children. They seized him and served him in like manner. Oh, what a scene for a man of Christian feeling to behold dead bodies strewed about the settlement in every direction and hung up at every native's door, their entrails taken out and thrown aside and the women preparing ovens to cook them. By great persuasion we prevailed on the savages not to cook any inside the fence or come into our houses during the time they were regaling themselves on what they termed sumptuous food - far sweeter, they said, than pork......

Another instance of their depravity was to make a musket ramrod red hot, enter it in the lower part of the victim's belly and let it run upwards, and then make a slight incision in a vein to let his blood run gradually, for them to drink." [14]

After returning to the place some time later Sheridan noted, "I observed that the enemy had formed three different settlements, and in each of them was a heap of bones similar to the first I had seen, and also to each a rack laced along the spot where they eat their victuals; on it they place the heads of their unfortunate victims that they may continually keep the objects of their revenge in their sight and mind, which is the continued bloodthirsty practice of this disgraceful race, whose constant study is meditating the death of their fellow-countrymen." [15]

Not all the victims were from the losing side in a battle for, as might be expected, such an unnatural and disgusting practice tended to form a life of its own. In the words of an early visitor to New Zealand, Mr. Earle, "We ran towards the fire and there stood a man occupied in a way few would wish to see. He was preparing the forequarters of a human body for a feast. The large bones having been taken out, were thrown aside, and the flesh being compressed, he was in the act of forcing it into the oven. While we stood transfixed by this horrible sight a large dog, which lay before the fire, rose up, seized the bloody head and walked off with it into the bushes, no doubt to hide it for another meal.

In this instance it was no enemy's blood to drink; there was no warrior's flesh to be eaten. They had no revenge to gratify; no plea could they make of their passions having been aroused in battle, nor the excuse that they ate their enemies to perfect their triumph. This was an act of unjustifiable cannibalism. Atoi, the chief who had given orders for this cruel feast, had only the night before sold us four pigs for a few pounds of powder." [16]

Describing the process, Mr. Earle continued, "After the head is taken off, the artist proceeds to open the breast, and the heart forms a delicate morsel. A longitudinal cut is then made from the shoulders to the wrists, which are cut crossways, leaving the hands hanging. The three bones of the arms are then taken out. The same is done from the thigh to the ankles, which are also cut crossways, leaving the feet hanging.

The leg bones are then extracted and the ribs, backbone, etc. are very neatly taken from the body, leaving nothing but flesh, with the exception of small bones in the hands and feet. These last are then scorched over the fire until the skin comes off, and it is then in a fit state to put in the *umu*. When done sufficiently it is taken out and parcelled to those who are to partake. The flesh when thus done of a full grown person is as coarse as horse flesh, the fat yellow, like that of Welsh mutton, and it has a skin or rather a rind, like a pig, but of a savoury smell. After the Maori knowledge of firearms, the skin of the buttocks of the men - generally tattooed - was taken off the body to make covers for cartouche boxes." [17]

When the *Lord Rodney* returned to Wellington on 20th November, 1835, it was found that during her absence the natives "had also killed several dogs....The savages also killed a young girl of about twelve years of age, cut her to pieces and hung her flesh up to posts in the same manner as the dogs". [18]

White people were not immune either. In the words of Dr. Felix Maynard and Alexandre Dumas in their book, *The Whalers,* "There is not a bay, not a cove, in New Zealand which has not witnessed horrible dramas, and woe to the white man who falls into the New Zealanders' hands." [19]

"In 1821 a vessel called the *General Gates* left Boston on a sealing voyage. On the 10th August following, five men and a leader, named Price, were landed near the south-west cape of the Middle [South] Island for the purpose of catching seals. Within six weeks the success of the men amounted to 3,563 skins, which had been salted and made ready for shipment.

One night, about eleven o'clock, their cabin was surrounded by a horde of natives, who broke open the place and made the Americans prisoners. The flour, salt provisions and salt for curing skins were all destroyed as their use and value were unknown to the savages.

After setting fire to the cabin and everything else that was thought unserviceable, they forced the sealers to march with them for some days to a place known by the name of Looking Glass Bay, to the north of Caswell Sound....The only food they had was roasted fish.....The natives then took John Rawton and, having fastened him to a tree, they beat in his skull with a club. The head of the unfortunate man was cut off and buried in the ground; the remaining part of the body was cooked and eaten.....The five survivors were made fast to trees, well guarded by hostile natives, and each day one of the men was killed by the ferocious cannibals and afterwards devoured, viz. James White and William Rawton of New London in Connecticut, and William Smith of New York. James West of the same place was doomed to die also but the night previously a dreadful storm, accompanied by thunder and lightning, frightened the natives away, and the two remaining Americans found means to unfasten the flax cords that bound them. At daybreak next morning they launched a small canoe that was within reach, and put to sea without any provisions or water, preferring death in this way to the horrid fate of their comrades." [20] Mercifully they were rescued by a trading vessel, the *Margery*.

In 1834 the whaling vessel, *Harriet*, was wrecked on the coast near Cape Egmont. Those on board - John Guard, his wife Betty, children John and Louisa, and crew (two Mates and 23 ordinary seamen) - reached the shore safely where they made tents out of the ship's sails. Two days later a local tribe made a dawn attack on them and two of the crew were killed, cut up and eaten. Others were taken prisoner, including Mrs. Guard and her children.

John Guard managed to escape in one of the *Harriet's* small boats. He went to Cloudy Bay and thence to Sydney to seek help. *HMS Alligator* and the New South Wales government schooner, *Isabella*, made haste for New Zealand. In fear of the warship's guns the Maoris gave up eight of the crew who, in their own words, were "eaten up with vermin, half starved, nearly naked, and our lives in hourly danger". [21]

Mrs. Guard and her daughter were then given up in return for the release of a local chief, Oaoiti, who had been captured by the sailors and held on the *Alligator*. She had been in the hands of the natives for five months, during which time she witnessed them killing and eating several of the captives, including her own brother.

"Few New Zealanders [Maoris] confidently expected to die in peace full of life. Some member at least of almost every family was killed and eaten. It was the fate of the race. Some who were not slain in battle were the victims of surprise. Each generation of each *hapu* and family had a feud to remember and avenge.....There was no security for life within the pa nor without it," wrote Sherrin and Wallace in their book, *The Early History of New Zealand.* [22]

This was also the view of Samuel Marsden, "I have met with no family but some branches of it had been killed in battle and afterwards eaten. If any chief falls into the hands of a tribe which he has oppressed and injured by the chance of war, they are sure to roast and eat him; and, after devouring his flesh, they will preserve his bones in the family as a memento of his fate, and convert them into fish hooks, whistles and ornaments. The custom of eating their enemies is universal. The origin of it is now too remote to be traced. The natives generally speak of it with horror and disgust, yet they expect that this will be their own fate in the end, as it has been with their forefathers and friends." [23]

Cannibalism was more widespread among the Maoris than elsewhere. It was a stain not only on New Zealand but on humanity itself. If Christianity and colonisation had imparted to these savage islands nothing but the ending of cannibalism, that would be full justification for introducing them.

The introduced railways made it easier for all New Zealanders to travel around. In the words of the former rebel chief, Rewi Maniapoto, on the King Country railway, "Tell Mr. Bryce [the Minister of Native Affairs] to hasten on the railway. I am an old man now and I should like to ride in the railway before I die".

Peter Churchman *Joe Williams* *Susan Glazebrook*

These judges are sneakily trying to introduce "tikanga" into the law on the false assumption that it was the system of law in New Zealand prior to 1840. Tikanga was never a system of law - just a mindset and a few customs that varied from time to time, from place to place, and from tribe to tribe. This new notion of tikanga undermines the common law rights that New Zealanders have enjoyed since 1840. See pages 86-95.

Oak trees in Ormond Road, Hastings. See Page 101.

Wellington harbour in the 21st century. When the Wakefields bought Wellington from chiefs Te Puni, Wharepouri and others in 1839 there was only one white man living there, Joe Robinson. With its large, landlocked harbour, the enterprise of the New Zealand Company and the energy of the pioneer settlers, this, the Mother City of New Zealand, developed rapidly under the impact of colonisation.

Some of our observers

Rev. William Williams

Edward Jerningham Wakefield

F.E. Maning

Rev. James Buller

CHAPTER 15

PROPERTY RIGHTS

Rights underpin the peaceful, secure ownership of land or anything else. A "right" is only a right if it can be enforced at law. If it can't be, then it is not a genuine right. As Thomas Jefferson wrote, "Nothing is ours, which another may deprive us of". [1]

Before 1840 any tribe or group of people in New Zealand could be deprived of whatever they had - or thought they had - by a stronger tribe with better weapons who might attack them during the night. In the Maori world might was right and no tribe or person could claim a right of possession that could be upheld at law because there was no law. Ownership or possession as of right was a concept foreign to Maori customs, in which it was decided solely by force of arms - so much so that they did not have a word for it.

As Peter Cresswell pointed out in the book, *Twisting the Treaty*, "In reality Maori actually owned nothing at all before Europeans arrived. Not New Zealand, not the land on which they lived or hunted, not even the things with which they had mixed their labour.....The country's natural resources had been all but stripped bare by slash and burn agriculture - stripped bare because, without secure property rights, there was no incentive to maintain those resources....Without security, domestic cultivation was extremely difficult." [2] If, for example, a tribe went away for a few days from their kumera patch, when they returned they might find it occupied by a stronger tribe and there was nothing they could do about it. Just like a family flying to Sydney for a week in the 21st century and, upon their return, finding their house or farm occupied by others and no longer in their possession or ownership.

"We observed some plantations of coomeras and potatoes belonging to Benee and his tribe; these were not contiguous to any village or habitation, and I consider it a great proof of the insecurity in which these people live that their grounds are rarely cultivated to any extent in the immediate vicinity of those places where they reside in congregated bodies....This is most certainly occasioned by that state of disunited barbarism and feudal enmity in which the different tribes reside among each other; who, having no moral institutions but resorting on all occasions to physical strength.....But this casual plan of cultivation is, however, disadvantageous to the regular improvement of the island; and could the tribes be brought to live in amity with each other and build their villages on the fertile grounds, their respective districts would in a short time assume a much more civilised appearance," wrote John Nicholas of his visit to New Zealand in 1814-5.[3]

When European settlers first came to New Zealand Taranaki was deserted because, in the words of Professor Keith Sinclair in his *History of New Zealand*, "in the 1820s, after many of the local Maoris had migrated to Otaki and Cook's Strait, the Waikato tribes had killed or enslaved all the rest." [4]

As Peter Cresswell pointed out, "Those Taranaki Maoris who fled the slaughter - and who had thereby avoided being killed, eaten or enslaved - only began to arrive back in Taranaki once it was safe to do so. What made it safe was the rule of law - the protection of individual rights that British law once did so well. The rule of law was a great gift to Taranaki Maoris; it quite literally saved their lives. One would like to think that those Taranaki Maoris alive to-day who are un-enslaved, uneaten and flourishing under the remnants of that rule of law would sometimes give thanks to its inception." [5]

Auckland also was too dangerous because it was such a desirable and convenient place to live and so any tribe that put a stake in the ground there could expect to be attacked by another tribe. "Imagine! Empty because they [the slopes of Mount Eden] were desirable. Why so? Because of the absence of property rights. Without secure property rights it just wasn't safe to be in a place where everyone wanted to be!....But in a culture where ownership is held by conquest rather than by right, having everything means that you very soon have nothing - because someone else wants it, and who gets to keep it is he who has the biggest friends." [6]

In the words of Rev. William Williams, writing of Auckland just after it was founded by Governor Hobson in 1840, "In the vicinity of Waikato and the Thames there sprang up the town of Auckland, in a locality which just before had been an unoccupied waste. No natives were living within many miles, for their mutual quarrels had separated the tribes and driven them far away into their own fastnesses for security. The novelty of a civilised community, where the houses, the mode of living, and everything belonging to them was strange, could not fail to draw together all who could go and witness the sight.

Then, too, it was found that the white man had many wants which the natives could supply. Their agricultural produce, pork, fish, firewood, and even bundles of grass all commanded a good price, which was soon exchanged for such commodities as would conduce to the natives' comfort. Manual labour was also much in demand, and thus many located themselves in the neighbourhood of the town until they had earned enough to secure for themselves some much-desired treasure." [7]

"Before the introduction of Christianity that district [Manukau] had been for many years deserted but, when there was no longer a fear of attack from Ngapuhi, the different tribes returned to their own localities. After this the colonisation of the country gave value to land which had before been useless, and hence each tribe was ready to secure to itself all that it could claim." [8]

"As soon as the fear of these incursions was removed the inhabitants became scattered in small parties and every man was able to reap the fruit of his own labour without molestation. One natural consequence was a great increase of agriculture, which was promoted by the demand for wheat in the English [settler] towns. In their purely native state every family had within itself its own resources. Their food, their clothing, their habitations, were all provided by the different members of the family; and the only interchange in the way of barter was in the purchase of canoes and the finer kinds of mats, which were made in perfection by a few only of the tribes. But now, in proportion to the facility of obtaining the coveted articles of foreign clothing and agricultural implements, the New Zealander was stimulated to raise twice as much produce as he required for his own consumption; and by traffic he supplied his wants at a much easier rate," wrote Rev. Williams. [9]

It was largely because of the pre-1840 insecurity of ownership that certain smart and far-sighted chiefs came to realise that whatever they had would be better protected by British law than by the law of the jungle in which they were living. As Chief Duatarra told Samuel Marsden and John Nicholas in 1814, "New Zealand man [native] is no fool". [10] The problem was that no one could utilise their land - certainly not in the long term - unless it was protected by law in a proper system of law.

"In the absence of any conception of property rights Maori culture had stripped bare the environmental resources that sustained their survival and left valuable land bare precisely because it was valuable....... It was a culture whose machinery was killing those trapped within. What saved them were the 'rights and privileges of British subjects' guaranteed to them by Article Three of the Treaty [of Waitangi]. Chief among these rights and privileges were property rights, bringing blessings previously unknown to this warrior culture." [11]

Thus for the first time in their history Maori now had property rights over their tribal lands that were recognised by law; before that their occupation had been in the nature of squatters. The new, legally enforced concept of fee simple gave them the right to do various things with it, including selling it for cash so that they could buy and enjoy some of life's comforts. The large scale sale of Maori lands that followed showed that any so-called "spiritual" link that they might have had for their hills and valleys and plains was less than their eagerness for the cash that they could spend at their will. "The Maoris themselves desired to part with their land to the Pakehas," declared a message from Ngapuhi to the Kohimarama conference of chiefs in 1860. [12]

And Rev. Buller: "The natives desired the settlement of Europeans among them as the only way of obtaining those articles of foreign merchandise which they needed....The Government was not so ready to buy, as were the natives to sell...Disappointed land buyers were vexed, native land sellers were disappointed" [13] and "At that time [c. 1840] there was a general desire to sell land to European residents; in all directions native chiefs were offering territory in exchange for foreign wares". [14]

It should be remembered that, although New Zealand was short of a lot of things in the nineteenth century, land was not one of them. It extended as far as the eye could see through the thick bush, unbridged rivers and scarcity of roads. The Maoris had more land than they needed or could cultivate - the whole of the South Island for about 2,000 natives. They lacked the organisational skills of the Europeans for large scale farming and so it is not surprising that they sold so much to the land hungry settlers who had to have somewhere to live and, with the good old Protestant work ethic, were prepared to put in the hard yards of turning their acres - and the country - into something more useful and valuable than endless hills of native bush and fern.

Native land was bought - usually by the Government - at a price agreed by the parties. In selling so much of their land the natives knew that the ensuing development would increase the value of the land that they kept - as it did.

The only lands that were taken by the Crown without payment were of those tribes who took part in the Kingite rebellion in the 1860s. When deciding to take up arms against the Government they knew that confiscation of their lands would be a likely consequence as the New Zealand Settlements Act 1863 provided for the legal confiscation of lands belonging to tribes that were taking part in hostilities against the Government.

Such loss of land after military defeat would have been familiar to the rebelling tribes as, in the earlier inter-tribal wars, the lands of the losers were invariably taken by the victor. The loss of some of their lands to the Government was a far less severe outcome of their war-making than in the earlier period when, in addition to losing their lands, they would have been killed, cooked and eaten as well.

In the words of Sir Apirana Ngata, "[By the Treaty of Waitangi] the Government placed in the hands of the Queen of England the sovereignty and the authority to make laws. Some sections of the Maori people violated that authority. War arose from this and blood was spilled. The law came into operation and land was taken in payment. This itself is a Maori custom - revenge, plunder to avenge a wrong. It was their own chiefs who ceded that right to the Queen. The confiscations cannot therefore be objected to in the light of the Treaty." [15] A major purpose of the confiscation was for the Government to be compensated for the enormous cost of the rebellion to the infant and not overly rich colony.

Statistics of the Confiscations after the Maori War of the 1860s [16]

Area	Original Confiscation (in acres)	Amount returned to natives or purchased from them	Final Confiscation (in acres)
Taranaki	1,275,000	813,000 (64%)	462,000
Waikato	1,202,172	314,364 (26%)	887,808
Tauranga	290,000	240,250 (83%)	49,750
Bay of Plenty (excluding Tauranga)	448,000	230,600 (51%)	211,060 *

The figures for the Bay of Plenty do not exactly match as 6,340 acres had been sold privately before confiscation.

In the event the Government confiscated lands as seen in the table. As can be seen, the Crown returned part of the land, depending on the behaviour of the tribes. Most of the confiscated land was returned to Ngaiterangi in the Tauranga area in recognition of the civilised way that they had behaved during the fighting in 1864 at Gate Pa where, unlike the primitive Ngatiruanui tribe in Taranaki, they did not desecrate the bodies of the fallen British soldiers. The eventual confiscation of only 49,750 acres in Tauranga was smaller than the size of some sheep stations such as Akitio, on the coast east of Dannevirke (90,000 acres), and Craigieburn (100,000 acres) and Cheviot Hills (87,478) acres in Canterbury.

On the other hand a much smaller proportion was returned in Waikato because the King movement there refused several generous offers proposed by the Government - in 1875, 1876, 1878, 1879, 1882, 1883 and 1888 - because Tawhiao, the defeated "Maori king", refused to swear an oath of loyalty to the Queen, which was part of the deal.

Of the confiscated lands in the Waikato some 90,000 acres between the Waikato and Piako Rivers were swamp lands of no earthly value to man or beast - apart from a few ducks, pukeko and other birds. However, the government and settlers got to work with drains, pumps and other machinery so that by 1881 around 20,000 acres of this confiscated marshland was "now in grass and carrying between 3,000 and 4,000 cattle." [17] In later years a lot more of this swamp was drained for agriculture. This could never have happened under tribal ownership. The new farms provided employment opportunities for local natives.

Having said all this, it should be pointed out that in the confusion of the times when there was not a lot of difference between "friendly" Maoris and hostile ones, there were in a few cases confiscation from tribes who had not been in actual rebellion. These tribes have since been compensated for such errors by modern Treaty settlements.

Thus, when the tribal elite and their supporters in Stuff News and other media outlets bleat about "Maori land loss" since 1840, they are, except for the relatively small amount of legally confiscated land from hostile tribes (above), talking about land that was willingly sold by the tribes for valuable consideration. It is like having a pioneer ancestor who had a big house in Parnell, Auckland, which was sold many years ago at the going rate, and the descendants in the 21st century bleat about "land loss" instead of acknowledging that their family had been paid for the property.

CHAPTER 16

INTRODUCTION OF LAW

"That wonderful construction of good sense and good judgement".
Winston Churchill on English common law.

One of the things that Captain Cook noticed about the people of New Zealand was that they were "without any settled form of government". [1]

When Samuel Marsden and John Nicholas visited New Zealand in 1814-5 they too noticed the total lack of laws or a system of law. Of the natives' superstitions Nicholas wrote, "It serves them in **the absence of laws** as the only security for the protection of persons and property, giving them an awful sacredness which no one dares to violate." [2]

While staying at Kerikeri on his last visit to New Zealand in 1837 Marsden was approached by Wiremu Hau, a young chief who had succeeded Hongi. Hau presented the missionary with a letter, appealing for the establishment of some form of law in New Zealand. "Sir, will you give us a law. This is the purpose of my address to you.

First, if we say 'let the cultivation be fenced, and a man through laziness does not fence [and] should pigs get into his plantation, is it right for him to kill them? Do you give us a law in this matter.

Second, Again, should pigs get into fenced land, is it right to kill or rather to tie them until the damage they have done is paid for? Will you give us a law in this.

Third again, should the husband of a woman die and she afterwards wish[es] to be married to another, should the natives of unchanged heart bring a fight against us - would it be right for us to stand up to resist them on account of their wrongful interference? Will you give us a law in this also.

Fourth, Again, in our wickedness one man has two wives but, after he has listened to Christ, he puts away one of them and gives her to another man to wife. Now, should a fight be brought against us, are we in this case to stand up to fight? Give us a law in this.

Again, should two men strive, one with the other, give me a law in this. My mode is to collect all the people together and judge them for their unlawful fighting, and also for wrongfully killing pigs. Therefore I say that the man who kills pigs for trespassing on his plantation, having neglected to fence, ought rather to pay for the pigs so killed. Will you give us a law in this.

Sixth, but there is another. Should a man who is in the Church come in a fight against us. Give us a law in this. Another thing.....slaves exalting themselves against their masters. Will you give us a law in this also." [3]

From this discussion it was obvious that the concept of law was something that the natives were ignorant of but wanted to learn about. This fits in with what Rev. J. Buller wrote of them. "**Their own rude law had been one of brute force.**" [4]

"Without the aid of iron the most trifling tool or utensil could only be procured by an enormously disproportionate outlay of labour in its construction and, in consequence, became precious to a degree scarcely conceivable by people of civilised and wealthy countries. This great value attached to personal property of all kinds increased proportionally the temptation to plunder; and, **where no law existed or could exist** of sufficient force to repress the inclination, every man as a natural consequence became a soldier......

Their intelligence causes them theoretically to acknowledge the benefits of law, which they see established amongst us; but their hatred of restraint causes them practically to abhor and resist its full enforcement amongst themselves.....people to whom, for their own safety and their preservation, we must give new laws and institutions," wrote F.E. Maning,[5] who also said, "At the time I am speaking of [pre-1840] the only restraint on such people [violent ones] was the fear of retaliation." [6]

"The disunited state of the tribes and their jealousy of each other **render it impossible to enact laws,**" wrote Captain Hobson to Governor Bourke of New South Wales after visiting New Zealand in 1837 on *HMS Rattlesnake.* [7]

"Pre-February, 1840, with **no law and order**, New Zealand was literally in a state of anarchy. Without law there could not be property rights; property could be taken and you could be killed without consequence," wrote Andy Oakley in his book, *Once We Were One.* [8] And John Robinson in *When Two Cultures Meet; the New Zealand Experience:* "In the absence of any codified law or higher authority, **there was no rule of law,** no guarantee of safety. The response to a perceived wrong would be either to attack and thus to revenge that wrong, or to face one another, starting with warlike challenges, or following with argumentative dispute." [9]

In 1842 Te Whero Whero, who later became the first Maori "king", speaking of the changes brought about by the Treaty of Waitangi, said to his people at Kaitohe, "And now I bring you this new treasure. **We have brought law**, a new law, to save us from killing and robbing each other. I will take this, my treasure, up Waipa, through every bend in the river. Friends, do not think little of what I say." [10]

"**It was the law of Christianity that put an end to our cannibal practices,**" Tamihana Te Rauparaha told the Kohimarama conference of chiefs in 1860. [11] Another chief, Hapurona Tohikura of Ngatiapa told the same conference, "My heart embraced the laws of the Pakeha....**The law put an end to our evils.**" [12] And Wiremu Te Whero of Ngatinaho: "**The Governor came, bringing with him the laws**". [13]

Himiona (Tuhourangi, Tarawera) told the same conference, "**After this came the law.** I saw its benefit and adopted it forthwith. The reason why I approved of it was a means of correcting all that went wrong." Pererika: "Missionaries were sent to us, and **then the Law appeared**". [14]

In the words of Sir Apirana Ngata, probably the greatest mind that Maoridom has produced and whose face adorns the current $50 note, "Many claims were made [pre-1840] by various Europeans for the one piece of land sold to each of them by various Maori chiefs. **Where was the law in those times to decide what was right?**.....The Maori did not have any government when the European first came to these islands. There was no unified chiefly authority over man or land...... How could such an organisation as a Government be established under Maori custom?" [15]

"They [the natives] regarded with admiration the peacefulness established by our habits of law and order, and displayed an almost unhoped-for degree of good temper in yielding their assent to the new order of things, which forbade the infliction of summary punishment as vengeance by the offended party according to their former customs," wrote Edward Jerningham Wakefield. [16]

It was certainly an improvement on their "former customs"; a dispute between two chiefs in Northland pre-1840 resulted in a hearing at the house of one of them. In the words of F.E. Maning, "The arguments on both sides were very forcible; so much so that in the course of the arbitration our chief and thirty of his principal witnesses were shot dead in a heap and sixty others badly wounded, and my friend's house and store blown up and burnt to ashes." [17]

In view of these many and largely eye-witness accounts that there was neither laws nor a system of law in New Zealand prior to the Treaty of Waitangi it is both astounding and alarming to record that there are forces in the current Maori sovereignty movement and its supporting cast that propagate the utterly false statement that there was a system of law in New Zealand prior to the Treaty.

Among the worst offenders are two judges of the Supreme Court of New Zealand, Joe Williams and Susan Glazebrook. Williams is the first part-Maori judge of this, the highest court in the land since the Labour government of Helen Clark so unwisely ended our age-old right of appeal to the Judicial Committee of the Privy Council in London - a more objective and competent court than the gimcrack institution that replaced it. Williams is a former chairman of the Waitangi Tribunal, where he "distinguished" himself by enthusiastically pushing the WAI 262 Report, recommending that ownership of all New Zealand's native plants and animals be taken away from the public and handed over to that small group of New Zealanders who can claim a smidgeon of Maoris blood. This Report is the epitome of racism, vengeance, nastiness and theft.

In a 2013 speech titled Lex Aotearoa, Williams "described *tikanga* Maori as Aotearoa's first law; for 700 years it governed society on our islands. When English colonisers imported their common law system - Aotearoa's second law - *tikanga* was mostly pushed aside. The Treaty of Waitangi was supposed to bring the two systems together." [18]

This is completely untrue. *Tikanga* was not a system of law before 1840. It was merely a word for the customs of various tribes and it differed from tribe to tribe, from place to place, and from time to time.

Tikanga was more a collection of cultural habits of these Stone Age people and it was heavily laced with revenge (*utu*), superstition (*tapu*), plunder (*muru*), violence and bloodshed. In an 1825 meeting at Kerikeri between missionaries and seven leading Ngapuhi chiefs Hongi Hika "described how the imperatives of *tikanga* prevented them from giving up war as a way of life." [19] Is this what Williams wants? A "system of law" *tikanga* certainly was not. It did not have courts, cases, precedents, clarity or consistency. Or even writing!!!

"We do not want to share the failure of current law, where key words such as *tikanga* shift around, with **the meaning chosen according to the requirements of a Maori litigant.** It is poor law when groups can plunder the public purse behind a smokescreen of ambiguous language," wrote Dr. John Robinson in *When Two Cultures Meet; the New Zealand Experience.* [20]

And as for Wiliams saying that the Treaty of Waitangi was meant to bring this non-law system of *tikanga* together with the common law; that is not only false but utterly preposterous as the whole point of the Treaty was to bring to New Zealand a system of law that hitherto it had not had. There is not a single word in the Treaty or its Preamble that states or even implies that *tikanga* was to have any place in the new British colony. Even if *tikanga* was a "system of law", it could not co-exist with English common law since it is not possible to have two different systems of law operating side by side in the same jurisdiction.

Despite being ruled by the same monarch since 1603 and being the same nation since the Act of Union of 1707 England and Scotland have different systems of law - the common law in England and an amalgam of common law and Roman law in Scotland. Completely separate jurisdictions. No one has ever tried to run them together as that would never work. It would work even less were English common law in New Zealand to run side by side with the non-law system of *tikanga*, which is not much more than the primitive practices and beliefs of pre-1840 tribal witch doctors.

In making the false assertion that *tikanga* was a system of law Williams was either woefully ignorant of the law, history and constitution of New Zealand or he was being deliberately deceitful - perhaps in pursuit of an agenda that seeks to undermine our common law rights that everybody in New Zealand has enjoyed since 1840. In either of these events it is questionable as to whether Williams is a fit and proper person to be a lawyer, let alone a judge.

Williams tried to introduce the fiction of *tikanga* in the Peter Ellis case in the Supreme Court and was supported in his error by another judge, Susan Glazebrook. And, just as cancer spreads, so too does this judicial falsehood that *tikanga* was a pre-1840 "system of law".

In the High Court case of *Edwards* (claims by tribes for large swathes of foreshore and seabed in the eastern Bay of Plenty) Judge Peter Churchman ignored the clearly stated intention of the democratically elected Parliament of New Zealand by putting the non-law *tikanga* above the requirement in the Marine and Coastal Area Act (s. 58) that a claimant must prove that its members have "exclusively used and occupied their claimed area from 1840 to the present day".

"Up until the assertion of sovereignty by Great Britain in 1840 the sole system of law in New Zealand was *tikanga* Maori," he falsely asserted

before waffling on about the "earth mother" and the "sky father"......
"with the earth being created when these two were thrust apart by their children" and other such juvenile Maori witch-doctory which should have no place in a modern court of law. By basing his judgement on a fictional "system of law" that never existed Churchman's whole rotten judgement seems to be based on a lie.

Since the claimants could not succeed in accordance with the clearly stated words of the Act, that should have been the end of it. Instead, Churchman said, "The task for the court in considering whether the requirements of s. 58 (1) (a) of the Act have been met is therefore not to attempt to measure the factual situation against Western property rights or even the tests at common law for the establishment of customary land rights. The critical focus must be on *tikanga* and the question of whether or not the specified area was held in accordance with the *tikanga* that has been established."

He then passed the whole thing over to a couple of part-Maoris, Hiria Hape and Doug Hauraki, who are not part of the justice system but who have spent their careers in advancing Maori culture and Maori interests, as to whether these applicants, who failed to succeed under the Act, held their claim "in accordance with *tikanga*". So, why do we have judges on Churchman's salary of $471,100 plus *unbelievable* perks when the case can be more or less decided by two outsiders?

In the words of former judge, Anthony Willy, commenting on this ignorant and dangerous judgement, "It is simply not tenable to import spiritual beliefs and ancient codes of conduct into the fabric of the contemporary common law of New Zealand. The law must be certain." [21] In the not too distant past New Zealand had judges - like Judge Willy - who knew, understood and valued the law. Now we have types like Churchman who ignore the law and in the process take away the rights of the people of New Zealand so as to indulge the greedy claims of small, private groups of *iwi*. Churchman's mistake, if not outrage, was all based on the premise that *tikanga* was a system of law when it plainly was not.

Another deeply flawed judge who ties his flag to the non-law system of *tikanga* rather than to our tried and tested common law is Grant Powell who, before he became a judge was deeply involved in acting for claimants to the Waitangi Tribunal. One has to wonder whether he was the best choice to be the judge in the case of *Reeder and Others,* dated 12th October, 2021, which gave some tribal groups rights of customary marine title to the coast near Tauranga.

Powell also ignored the Marine and Coastal Area Act and said that the test of whether the claimants could prove exclusive use and occupation of the claimed area must be viewed "through a *tikanga* lens that reflects the continuity of customary relationship with the land" and that the nature of *tikanga* colours the words", thus allowing a lower threshold than in the Act. [22]

He really gave the game away and seems to have exposed his own bias when he said that the court must take a *protective* approach to customary rights and interpret these liberally in favour of indigenous groups (and against the rest of us). The Act does not say that. This judgement is every bit as dodgy as that of Churchman and does nothing to arrest the rapidly sinking trust in the judiciary by ordinary New Zealanders who have had their traditional rights shafted in so many ways by defective, if not biased, judges.

These four judges - Williams, Glazebrook, Churchman and Powell - are playing fast and loose with the law so as to advance the interests of one minority race group at the expense of all other New Zealanders. As John Robinson wrote in his book, *Regaining A Nation; Equality and Democracy,* "The whole basis of law is being overturned by judges who are effectively carrying out a coup d'etat against both the law and the constitution". The function of a judge is to apply the laws that are enacted by the democratically elected Parliament and **not** to make the law and certainly **not** to break the law. They need to be reminded of their proper function very forcefully if they are not to become the enemies of freedom and democracy.

In choosing to ditch *tikanga, utu* and other forms of violence, and embrace for the first time a system of law that provided enforceable personal and property rights, the chiefs of 1840 were acting wisely; in fact, they were going for the top prize in exchanging their Stone Age culture for the legal system of England that was the most advanced and civilised in the whole world and which placed more importance on individual rights and humane values than any other. The rigid Code Napoleon of France was not - and still is not - a better system than English common law while in 1840 the United States was still practising slavery and would do so for another quarter of a century. As Sir Apirana Ngata said in his speech at Waitangi on the centenary of the Treaty in 1940, "Let me acknowledge first that, in the whole world I doubt whether any native race has been so well treated by a European people as the Maori." [23]

It beggars belief that, after nearly two centuries of living successfully and prosperously under English common law, a clique of out-of-control judges like Churchman, Powell, Williams and Glazebrook should try to reverse the wisdom of the chiefs of 1840. By falsely insisting that *tikanga* was a "pre-1840 system of law."

In the words of John Robinson, "The Maori were fortunate that it was the British, at that time when the ideas of equality and universal humanity were flourishing, who were the dominant new force in the South Pacific. There were many people who would have used their superior weapons to kill them and take their land without a second thought, to conquer and enslave them (Cortez in Mexico, Pizarro in Peru and the Belgians in the Congo), slaughter them (as Alexander the Great did to all who opposed him, as Maori did in the Chathams). If we consider all societies throughout history - like the Spanish in the seventeenth century - the British were remarkably considerate." [24]

Article 3 of the Treaty of Waitangi gave all the people of New Zealand - native and settler - all the rights of British subjects and so liberated the natives from a state of fear and anarchy - something that Joe Williams, Susan Glazebrook, Churchman and Powell should be celebrating instead of trying to switch the clock back to a past that no one except those of ill-will could possibly want.

The rule of law not only guarantees individual rights such as habeas corpus and free speech but, through the law of contract, etc. has provided the foundation for the economic growth and improvement in living standards that have transformed New Zealand into the modern and comfortable society that we know today. As Apirana Ngata stated, "British law has been the greatest benefit bestowed by the Queen on the Maori people". [25] **Not tikanga**!

The facts are very simple. Before 1840 there were no laws or system of law in New Zealand; since 1840 all New Zealanders have lived under English law, the finest system of law yet conceived by man. It is a treasure that must be preserved.

CHAPTER 17

LANGUAGE

At the time of colonisation the native tribes of New Zealand spoke approximately thirteen dialects, some of which were mutually incomprehensible. Being Stone Age people, their vocabulary was limited (approximately 800 to 1,500) words but some words had several meanings. They had neither a written language nor any precise standard of measurement. Both of these were gifted to them by the missionaries and colonists.

In 1820 the missionary, Thomas Kendall, went to England with two Ngapuhi chiefs from Northland, Hongi Hika and Waikato. Kendall took them up to Cambridge where the noted linguist, Professor Samuel Lee, took note of their (Ngapuhi) pronunciations. From these he compiled a book entitled *A Grammar and Vocabulary of the Language of New Zealand*, which was published in England by the Church Missionary Society. This, the written Maori language, was the creation of an English professor at one of England's two great universities. As such, it was a gift to the Maoris.

"The chief benefit to be dreived from literacy lies in the development of imagination. This is not only unique to man, but is the greatest gift with which we have been provided. From imagination have come all the highest creative achievements of civilisation; in art, music, architecture, poetry and all the ennobling impulses of thought and belief." [1]

With this new dictionary the Bible and Prayer Book and other literary works were able to be translated into the Maori language. These books were printed on a printing press, that wonderful invention of the German, Johannes Gutenberg, in 1440, which transformed writing and much of the world. It was at the Paihia Mission in 1834 that New Zealand's first printing press was landed. It came with an operator, William Colenso, and printed the first book published in New Zealand.

However, the natives' ability to have their own language in writing was not the only benefit of colonisation in respect of language. The early whalers, sealers, missionaries and settlers who came to New Zealand were almost exclusively from English speaking countries - mainly Britain but also Australia and the United States (especially the whalers from Massachusetts and New York state). Thus did English quickly become the language of New Zealand and the natives were keen and quick to learn it.

When schools were set up by the new colonial government in native areas the locals were very keen that they be taught in English. For example, when the Governor of New Zealand, Sir George Bowen visited Taupo in April, 1872, the local chiefs, Poihipi Tukairangi and Reweti Te Kume, begged him to build a school there where "their children might learn the language and arts of the English". [2]

In the words of Chief Reweti Te Kume, "Taupo is yours.....to carry out the work of the Europeans: to make roads and other works and to have schools to teach our children English". [3]

This was the desire of many Maoris; they wanted their children to go to school and be taught in English and not Maori. "In the 1870s, shortly after the Native Schools system was established, a number of prominent Maori sought through Parliament to place greater emphasis on the teaching of English in the schools. A newly elected Maori Member of Parliament, Tomoana, sought legislation to ensure that Maori children were taught only in English. Several petitions in a similar vein were also taken to Parliament by Maori." [4]

Thus were Maoris brought within the English speaking world and today are natural speakers of the world's most widely used language - one that is the first language of more than fifty countries, mostly ex-British colonies, and the richest language in poetry and drama.

From colonisation they scored a "double first": their own tongue in writing and a new English language.

CHAPTER 18

FAUNA AND FLORA

"The new settlers brought gorse for hedges, fast growing trees for timber, fruit trees, nut trees, wheat, oats, barley and clover."

New Zealand's Changing Biodiversity, Jim Hilton and Roger Childs. [1]

The native people were not the only life form in New Zealand at the time that the first Europeans arrived; there were also the birds and the trees and the plants, and it is respect of the impact that colonisation made upon the environment that the benefits are offset in several ways by the disadvantages.

By 1800 the land of New Zealand had already been ravaged by the Maoris who, "with fire, dogs [*kuri*] and hunting weapons",[2] had already exterminated all nine species of moa as well as 38 species of birds (including the Haast's eagle, adzebill, the giant goose, the flightless Fisher's duck and all but one of the flightless wrens) as well as three species of frogs, numerous lizards, a bat and the New Zealand sea lion and sea elephant.[3] Others, like the huia, were on the point of extinction and, in fact, became extinct shortly after the Europeans' arrival. The Maoris had also burned about 40% of the forest, mainly on the lowlands of the east coast of both islands.

In the words of W.F. Benfield in his book, *The Third Wave; Poisoning the Land*, "By around 1500 A.D. the expansion phase of the Maori invasion was complete. A stable ecosystem, that had evolved over millions of years through many climate epochs without significant outside influence, was irretrievably lost. In its place was a human society without the technology to support the population that had grown on the moa and other birds.....An extremely destructive phase in the evolution of this Gondwana land remnant was drawing to a close. A new player was entering the scene, one who would bring his own problems, but for the Maoris it would save them from the further consequences of environmental ruin with its resulting food shortage, social collapse and warfare." [4]

Into this already partly ravaged environment stepped the Europeans with their own birds, trees, flowers and farm animals, even earthworms. "It was only natural that our first settlers wanted to bring animals and plants from their native countries to New Zealand. Maori brought rats and dogs. Europeans brought rabbits, possums, pigs, goats and highly prized hunting animals like deer, chamois and tahr. They also brought game birds for hunting: quail, pheasant, Canadian geese and mallard ducks.

The kiore rat had arrived with the Maoris when they sailed their canoes from Polynesia in the thirteenth century and, despite being a food source for them, it was reasonably rampant by the time that the European settlers arrived in the 1840s. When a family from Bath, England, arrived in Wellington on the *Birman* in March, 1842, the wife wrote home, "On getting ashore we found that the building intended for our use and accommodation had been appropriated by a shipload of emigrants who had had the good fortune to arrive a few days before we did. The result was that we were all crammed into a large, empty storehouse - just like an old barn, filthy beyond description and overrun with swarms of small rats [the small, brown kiore]." [5]

However, it wasn't long before the kiore rat was progressively reduced in numbers by various factors, including the introduction of the cat which itself was to become a predator. However, the kiore rat was more than replaced by the Norway rat and the ship rat which, like the cockroaches, infested every wooden ship that sailed the Seven Seas.

Since the arrival of the European a further eighteen species of bird (including snipe, saddleback and the Stephens Island wren) have disappeared although, as already noted, several of these were already on the verge of extinction. The Europeans brought with them the concept of conserving species with the result that sanctuaries were set up at such places as Little Barrier Island (1894), Stephens Island (1896) and Kapiti Island (1897)

Gorse was introduced in 1835 by the missionaries and, as it spread down the country, was soon to become a prolific, unwanted and noxious plant. Then the first Saint Andrew's Day of settler New Zealand was celebrated on 30 November, 1840, in Wellington. "They planted the first thistle in New Zealand at Mr. Lyon's farm on the Wellington side of Petone." [6] After that came an even worse one - blackberry - which has been the bane of gardeners and farmers ever since.

Initially Captain Hobson wanted a moratorium on the felling of kauri but he was persuaded by Tamati Waka Nene and other northern chiefs to let the felling go ahead as they were making money out of it. With their efficient metal saws the pioneers cut down much of the kauri and totara trees in the North Island. This was done out of sheer necessity for, like every other colony or country, New Zealand had to pay its bills. Before farming became a major exporter in the 1880s New Zealand had to export whatever the rest of the world wanted in order to get the overseas funds to pay for the imports of such things as machinery, consumer goods and coal, the last mentioned coming mainly from Newcastle, New South Wales. And what the Australians wanted was kauri as it was the only timber that was impervious to that scourge of Australian builders, the white ant, not to mention its desirability for the masts and spars of wooden sailing vessels. Throughout the nineteenth century kauri and its gum were the main contributors to New Zealand's wealth, providing employment for thousands and export revenue of millions.

Just as the Maoris resisted Hobson's proposed moratorium on the cutting of kauri so too did they ignore a Notice issued by Edward Shortland, Private Secretary to the Governor, in 1842. The Notice was: "The Governor further directs it to be notified that any person cutting timber or firewood on the reserves and especially on the belt which surrounds the town of Wellington, will be proceeded against according to the law".

"The Maoris, in utter disregard of the published notice of the Governor, did some three months ago fell large quantities of trees, and are now employed in burning them off the ground. An immense number of trees not cut down have been blackened and blighted by the smoke and, unless a stop is put to their proceedings, the Maoris will succeed in converting the chief beauty of our town into a mass of cheerless, stunted, naked barrenness. There is but one feeling of sorrow and anger on this subject among the settlers. We are aware of the difficulty in enforcing the law against the Maoris," wrote the *New Zealand Gazette and Wellington Spectator* on 19th January, 1842.

Not all of the European introductions were bad. Worms and bees were a great aid to farming while the sheep, cows, pigs and goats were to form the basis of the economy. In the words of Jim Hilton and Roger Childs in their book, *New Zealand's Changing Biodiversity*, "Basically humans got it right with most of its biota imports. Present day New Zealand is richer in biodiversity than it was before humans arrived. People use many exotic species to make money and pay their bills.

The beauty of many of these non-natives enhances our surroundings and makes our country more attractive - the blossom trees of Cambridge and Alexandra, the tall poplars between Wanganui and Raetihi, the phoenix palms along Kennedy Road in Napier, the Norfolk pines that grace Wellington's Oriental Parade, the oaks that shade Hastings' Ormond Road, and the weeping willows that stretch down to the waters of the Avon in Christchurch.....The trout in our lakes and rivers, as well as deer and other introduced animals, bring fishermen and hunters from overseas." [7]

And not just from overseas. In the words of fisherman and journalist, Tony Orman, "In New Zealand's egalitarian society anyone can fish or hunt. It was a legacy that the first European settlers instilled into the new colony in order to escape the feudal system of Britain where, for example, the best trout fishing, deerstalking or pheasant shooting is the preserve of the wealthy minority who could pay the exorbitant trout and salmon fishing, game bird shooting and deerstalking fees required." [8]

In 1842 the first pheasants arrived. "Mrs. Willis, who was a passenger in the *London*, deserves the thanks of the colony for having brought the first pheasants to New Zealand. A cock and three hens were landed in safety," wrote Edward Jerningham Wakefield. [9]

Even better was the feathered brigade on the *Cashmere*, which arrived at Auckland on 8th April, 1862, with 88 singing and other birds "whose carols are so grateful to the ears of the colonists and so fruitful of suggestions of home". [10] These birds included partridges, blackbirds, thrushes, skylarks, goldfinches, bullfinches, linnets, sparrows, starlings, Canadian geese, and teal. They were in 81 cages on the deck throughout the voyage and had been fed on German paste, preserved liver, rice, potatoes, carrots, wheat, apples, hemp seed and barley. They had been caught in the wild rather than being hand reared from the nest. Thus they had been at liberty and so should have been stronger and more able to look after themselves.

Deer came in 1861 with a stag and two hinds from Lord Petre of Thorndon Hall in Essex, after which the inner suburb of Wellington is named. "Within two years they had increased to seven animals and by 1870 the herd numbered more than seventy." [11] Trout were introduced in 1867 and so this dish could be added to venison as yet a further widening of the New Zealand menu.

As we know, not all the introductions were so positive. After rabbit numbers exploded the ferret was introduced on the grounds that rabbits are the desired diet of ferrets. Stoats and weasels came too and they didn't even have the justification of killing rabbits.

As W.F. Benfield pointed out in his book, *The Third Wave; Poisoning the Land,* "By the end of the nineteenth century the rate of importation and establishment of exotic life forms had reached the stage where you could say that a whole new ecosystem was being transplanted on to the old.....A land mass on which, a century before, the population was having to maintain itself by constant warfare and cannibalism was now able to export foodstuffs to the world." [12] In the process, despite hiccups along the way, natives and exotics have learned to live with each other - be they birds, trees, plants, insects or farm animals.

CHAPTER 19

POPULATION

It is difficult to assess the native population prior to census taking after 1840. In his authoritative book, *The Corruption of New Zealand Democracy,* Dr. John Robinson wrote, "The New Zealand Maori population had decreased considerably from 1800. After 1840, while the population decline continued, the rate of decline steadily decreased as the population stabilised, setting the scene for recovery by the end of the century.

While estimates (which could be described as guesstimates) vary considerably, reasonable estimates of the Maori population are 120,000 in 1800 and 70,000 in 1840. The 1857-8 census value (again with some uncertainty but much more definite) was 56,049. This declined further to 47,330 in 1874. Thereafter the Maori population stabilised (43,927 in 1886) and was growing in 1900".[1] The 1886 figure was the nadir of Maori numbers although that particular census (1886) is widely considered to have been defective. By 1891 the naive population was 44,177 and has risen ever since.

The decline in numbers between 1800 and 1840 is explained by the tens of thousands of deaths in the musket wars, as mentioned in the chapter on Tribal Warfare. Other - but very minor - contributory factors would have been infanticide, the poor health and hygiene in native communities, and diseases like measles, tuberculosis and influenza, which were contracted by natives' association with Europeans. However, there is no evidence that these imported diseases were a major cause of the decline in the native population although they would have made a contribution.

"When the natives became generally armed with the musket they at once abandoned the hills and, to save themselves the great labour and inconvenience occasioned by the necessity of continually carrying provisions, fuel and water to their precipitous hill-castles - which would be also, as a matter of necessity, at some inconvenient distance from at least some part of the extensive cultivations - descended to the low lands and there, in the centre of the cultivations, erected a new kind of fortification adapted to the capabilities of the new weapon. This was their destruction for they built their oven-like houses in mere swamps where the water, even in summer, sprang with the pressure of the foot, and where in winter the houses were often completely flooded.

There, lying on the spongy soil, on beds of rushes which rotted under them - in little, low dens of houses, or kennels, heated like ovens at night and dripping with damp in the day - full of noxious exhaltations from the damp soil and impossible to ventilate - they were cut off by disease in a manner absolutely frightful. No advice would they take; they could not see the enemy which killed them, and therefore could not believe the Europeans who pointed out the cause of their destruction.

This change of residence was universal, and everywhere followed by the same consequences, more or less marked. The strongest men were cut off and but few children were reared. And even now [1860s], after the dreadful experience they have had and all the continued remonstrations of their *pakeha* friends, they take but very little more precaution in choosing sites for their houses than at first; and when a native village or a native house happens to be in a dry, healthy situation, it is often more the effect of accident than design.....

Many other causes combined at the same time to work the destruction of the natives. Besides the change of residence from the high and healthy hill forts to the low grounds, there were the hardship, over-labour, exposure and half-starvation to which they submitted themselves - firstly, to procure these very muskets which enabled them to make the fatal change of residence, and afterwards to procure the highly and justly valued iron implements of the Europeans.

When we reflect that a ton of cleaned flax was the price paid for two muskets, and at an earlier date for one musket, we can see at once the amount of exertion necessary to obtain it. But supposing a man to get a musket for half a ton of flax, another half-ton would be required for ammunition; and in consequence, as every man in a native *hapu* of, say a hundred men, was absolutely forced on pain of death to procure a musket and ammunition at any cost, and at the earliest possible moment (for, if they did not procure them, extermination was their doom at the hands of those of their countrymen who had), the effect was that this small *hapu*, or clan, had to manufacture, spurred by the penalty of death, in the shortest possible time, one hundred tons of flax, scraped by hand with a shell, bit by bit, morsel by morsel, half-a-quarter of an ounce at a time.

Now as the natives, undisturbed and labouring regularly at their cultivations, were never far removed from necessity or scarcity of food, we may easily imagine the distress and hardship caused by this enormous imposition of extra labour. They were obliged to neglect their crops in a very serious degree, and for many months in the year were in a half-starving condition; working hard all the time in the flax swamps. The insufficient food, over-exertion and unwholesome locality killed them fast.

As for the young children, they almost all died; and this state of things continued for many years, for it was long after being supplied with arms and ammunition before the natives could purchase, by similar exertion, the various agricultural implements and other iron tools so necessary to them; and it must always be remembered, if we wish to understand the difficulties and over-labour the natives were subjected to, that while undergoing the immense extra toil, they were at the same time obliged to maintain themselves by cultivating the ground with sharpened sticks, not being able to afford to purchase iron implements in any useful quantity till the first great, pressing, paramount want of muskets and gunpowder had been supplied.

Thus continual excitement, over-work, insufficient food, exposure and unhealthy places of residence, together with a general breaking up of old habits of life, thinned their numbers; European diseases also assisted, but not to any very serious extent.

In the part of the country in which I have had means of observing with exactitude, the natives have decreased in numbers over one-third since I first saw them. That this rapid decrease has been checked in some districts, I am sure, and the cause is not a mystery.

The influx of Europeans has caused a competition in trading, which enables them to get the highest value for the produce of their labour, and at the same time has opened to them a hundred new lines of industry and afforded them other opportunities of becoming possessed of property. They have not at all improved these advantages as they might have done but are, nevertheless, as it were in spite of themselves, on the whole richer - i.e. better clothed, fed and in some degree lodged than in past years; and I see the plough now running where I once saw the rude pointed stick poking the ground," wrote F.E. Maning. [2]

"The growth or decay of a population is determined to a considerable extent by the initial demographic structure......Maori population loss in the decades following 1840 can be largely explained by the initial demographic structure, of few young and a lack of women, produced in the previous era.....The decline of the Maori population after 1840 was largely determined by events prior to 1840, which had given rise to a very poor initial age and gender distribution. The evidence further points to continuing female infanticide throughout the remainder of the nineteenth century." [3]

In other words, the decline in population that was happening up to 1840 - mainly as a result of the musket wars - did not suddenly stop with the arrival of British sovereignty in 1840 as if cured by a magic bullet. The shortage of female breeding stock continued for several more decades, aided by continuing but diminishing rates of infanticide. The new colonial government did as much as might be expected to improve Maori health (and thereby life expectancy) in spite of obstruction from the *tohungas* (not finally dealt with until the *Tohunga* Suppression Act of 1907) and the reluctance of various tribes and sub-tribes to wean themselves away from unhealthy living conditions and poor hygiene.

Eventually the benefits of Western health prevailed and from about 1900 onwards the Maori population increased steadily while their life expectancy is now about triple what it was in 1840. John Robinson summed it up neatly in his book, *When Two Cultures Meet; the New Zealand Experience*. "There was massive inter-tribal warfare in the first forty years of the nineteenth century. The disruption included the virtual disappearance of whole groups, with some lands left empty, the deaths of one third of the Maori population, the migration of many peoples and significant changes on Maori culture - beliefs, desires, behaviour. The population was left with a shortage of young and women, which determined the subsequent decline.....That initially poor population structure, together with subsequent low fertility and continuing high mortality, totally explains the population decline. The population was not significantly affected by the later wars (after 1840) and there is no evidence whatsoever of a demographic impact from loss of land." [4]

The loss of life in the Maori wars of the 1840s and 1860s was 2,154 on the rebels' side and 310 British and colonial troops plus around 250 *kaupapa* (friendly Maori). Adding the *kaupapa* to the dead rebels gives a total of Maori dead on both sides of 2,404 over the period 1840s-1870, which is a drop in the bucket compared with the death toll in the earlier musket wars (43,600 to 80,000). However, this is something that the Government and the Education Department do not want us to know, which is why the new school history curriculum (introduced 2023) ignores the inter-tribal wars and presents the later conflicts between Maori rebels and the lawful government as some sort of seminal event in the country's history with, of course, a narrative that invents massive cruelty on the part of the Crown forces such as the lie that in the skirmish at Rangiaowhia in the Waikato Maori women and children were burned in a church and that the government's peaceful occupation of Parihaka in 1881 was a "holocaust" when, in fact, the only injury was to a boy's toe when a trooper's horse accidentally trod on it.

These are nothing more than crude indoctrination sessions in the name of "history" which have as their purpose instilling in part-Maoris a sense of grievance and in European New Zealanders a sense of guilt so as to perpetuate division and ill-will in society. A true history of the country would make all students feel proud of what has been achieved in such a short time. Just as parents are allowed to exclude their children from sex education classes in schools, so too should they have the right to absent their children from these hate-filled indoctrination sessions in the name of "history".

The actual figures show that colonisation had an ameliorating impact on native demographics but only after the decline in numbers started to recede and, just as Rome was not built in a day, nor were these inherent obstructions to native population growth arrested quickly - not even in a generation. "Shortages of both breeding women and children (the next generation of breeders) created in the preceding period largely determined the inevitable population decline from 1840 onwards and until late in the century." [5] No society can lose at least a third of its population - as the Maoris did during the musket wars - and expect recovery immediately upon the cessation of that mass slaughter.

CHAPTER 20

WELCOME, WHITE MAN

The unfriendly reception that the natives of the East Coast gave to Captain Cook when he first stepped ashore in New Zealand on 8th October, 1769, was not by any means the norm. As the natives came to appreciate the products of Western invention as well as the profits that could accrue to them by trading with sailing ships, their attitude towards the white man became a lot more welcoming.

As early as 1814-5 John Nicholas wrote, "These people [a tribe in Northland], however they might dislike Europeans as occasional visitors, were nevertheless gratified with the idea of white men settling among them and becoming permanent inhabitants of their country." [1]

"In those days [pre-1840] the value of a *pakeha* to a tribe was enormous....A *pakeha* trader was of a value say about twenty times his own weight in muskets," wrote F.E. Maning. [2] "A great change had come over the Maori tribes. Alive to the advantages of trade, they wished for the arrival of white men," wrote Rev. J. Buller of the 1840 period. [3]

"From 1792 whalers and sealers were harvesting the rich southern ocean from bases in Riverton, Waikouaiti and Banks Peninsula, to name a few. Many led reasonably settled lives, taking Maori wives - some sold or given to them by chiefs anxious to protect their daughters from predatory northern tribes," wrote Bruce Moon in *One Treaty, One Nation*. [4]

From the beginning of settlement Europeans were seen as a useful factor in giving security to a tribe from its enemies. Edward Jerningham Wakefield wrote of the *Tory*, the first ship sent to New Zealand by the colonising New Zealand Company, as it sailed into Wellington harbour on 20th September, 1839. Two canoes arrived alongside with two local chiefs, Te Puni and his nephew, Wharepouri: "Te

Puni eagerly inquired the motive of our visit and expressed the most marked satisfaction on hearing that we wished to buy the place and bring white people to it. Wharepouri also expressed his willingness to sell the land, and his desire of seeing white men come to live upon it." [5] This was a few months before the Treaty of Waitangi brought law and order to the land.

So insecure were these Wellington natives in their occupation (one cannot say "legal title") that Wharepouri had been living for long periods on Somes Island in case of a land attack by Te Rauparahau from his haunt on Kapiti Island or by their traditional enemy, Ngati Kahungunu in the Wairarapa, who still had scores to settle. In fact, on 22nd September - only three days after the *Tory* arrived at Wellington, there was a direct threat to those Te Aitiawa living on the Kapiti coast from Te Rauparaha and it was such as to frighten the chiefs who were being entertained on the *Tory* that they "went ashore in defiance of a gale to gather the particulars and consult on means of defence."

Te Puni and Wharepouri, who had been to Sydney and so knew what a British settlement was like, would have known that the best protection against one's enemies was the presence of Europeans with their superior firearms and organisation. Hence their willingness to sell to the New Zealand Company much of Wellington - land that they decided they did not need. [6]

"We want," said they, "to live in peace, and to have white people come amongst us. We are growing old and we want our children to have protectors in people from Europe....We have long heard of ships from Europe. Here is one at length; and we will sell our harbour and land, and live with the white people when they come to us." [7]

The first ship to bring British settlers was the *Aurora* which, unlike the *Tory* (an exploratory vessel), unloaded 148 eager colonists on 22nd January, 1840, which day has ever since been celebrated as Wellington's Anniversary Day. John Wallace, one of the passengers, wrote, "It was a splendid morning. Mr. Richard Deighton, Samuel Deighton and myself were the first to land - opposite the native village at Petone - or 'end of the sand' from its position. We strolled a short distance to the edge of the bush observing, perched in one of the trees, several wood pigeons. Each of us at the same instant shot one of these fine birds. The first great object of attention and interest was the venerable old chief, Epuni [Te Puni]....together with sons and endless relatives and *pa* full of natives who were delighted to greet us with '*Kapia te pakeha*' (Welcome, white man)" [8]

It was the same further up the coast. "Colonel Wakefield, having visited Waikanae, was eagerly received by the missionary natives there, who offered to sell their land; but for no consideration except the munitions of war as they wished to defend themselves against the Ngati raukawa." [9]

In the words of the *New Zealand Gazette and Wellington Spectator* of 22nd December, 1842, writing of Colonel Wakefield's ride on horseback the 112 miles from Wanganui to Wellington, "All along the coast the native population appeared anxious to receive the White men; and Colonel Wakefield was pressed by the principal chiefs to send hundreds of settlers to reside among them."

The same paper reported on 12th January, 1842, "The natives all the way to the Manawatu showed by their acts how desirous they were to have the colonists of Port Nicholson settle among them. They complained that all the benefit they derived from the shipping at present was the amusement of seeing it pass through the straits [between Kapiti Island and the mainland].

When we arrived at the Ohau river at first a most unreasonable price was asked for carrying our large party across that stream. The belief was that we were proceeding to Wanganui; but when it was ascertained that we were proceeding to examine the Manawatu, orders were immediately given to take all over free of expense. At the Manawatu we were feasted at every potato ground at which we made a call, and canoes were provided and we were taken to examine land in the neighbourhood of the river, without payment being required.

Some of the chiefs journeyed with us and took the greatest pains to give us every information respecting the land, its productions and the river. The desire to know our opinion was unceasing, and as often as we answered them that the country was approved and would be occupied by the white men, so often did we afford them the highest satisfaction."

The same in the Wairarapa. "Robert Stokes' exploratory party of six men who left Hutt on 25th November, 1841, then descended into the Wairarapa to make a more detailed investigation and also to contact the local Maoris, who assured them that it would be well that the Pakeha should live among them if they received compensation for their land." [10]

And in the Hawkes Bay. "By the end of the 1840s reports were reaching Wellington of a fine tract of country waiting for settlement at Ahuriri. Maori chiefs were asking the government to send settlers. 'Send me Europeans for my land as soon as possible that we may have respectable European gentlemen. I am annoyed with the low Europeans of this place." [11]

When the *Jane Gifford* arrived with the founding stock of Scottish settlers for Auckland on 9th October, 1842, one of the passengers wrote, "A number of Maoris were standing on the beach and welcomed us to New Zealand. They all seemed glad to see us, shaking hands and talking in their own language." [12]

Not all welcomes were so straightforward. When the *Hodving* arrived at Napier on 1st December, 1873, with a shipful of Scandinavian settlers a certain local, Paora Rerepo "took the opportunity of testifying his loyalty as a British subject by striking up 'Rule Britannia' with more vehemence than talent. As he accompanied his singing with uncommonly hideous gestures and distortions, some of the female part of his audience seemed hardly to know what to think of it, and it was felt to be best to send him away. While the immigrants were on the wharf, however, he, together with Tareha and Paora Toki, took the opportunity again of showing their esteem by grasping the hands of their new friends in the most affectionate fashion." [13]

At Paparoa, on the Kaipara harbour, the Wesleyan missionary Rev. W. Gittos, "who had a thorough knowledge of the Maori mind and had secured the confidence of the natives, knew the danger which existed of tribal wars, and the Maoris in the Kaipara were in fear of invasion. Hence it was at the missionary's suggestion that they [the Maoris] released portions of land for occupation by British subjects, opening the way for a ring of European settlements in proximity to the Maoris, which would be a safeguard to the local natives from tribal interference." [14]

It was the same further down the Kaipara harbour. When the entrepreneurial John McLeod purchased 396 acres at Helensville (named after his wife) from Chief Te Otene in 1862 to set up a sawmill which provided employment to the local tribe, they were very happy. "They thought what an advantage it would be to them if they had a *pakeha* with them to do business," wrote McLeod's niece, Catherine Oxley. [15]

Even during and after the Kingite rebellion of the early 1860s a tribe still felt more secure if it were near a European settlement. In the words of Auckland's *Daily Southern Cross* of 17th August, 1864, "The great desire of the chiefs and their followers appears to be to fix their settlements as near as possible to the camp, or to any place where it may be surmised that a body of military settlers will have their farms. Having tendered their submission to the Queen's authority and being to all appearances earnestly desirous to remain in peaceful occupation of their lands, the old feeling seems returning to them of the necessity and advantage of having *pakeha* traders resident in their midst - with the new feeling superadded that a residence near a military camp is necessary for their personal safety from enemies of their own race who may not have seen sufficient cause so far to go and do likewise, but on the contrary threaten dire vengeance against their brethren for having succumbed before the heavy shocks of war which they have sustained."

In April, 1872, the Governor, Sir George Bowen, travelled to Taupo. In his address of welcome the local chief, Poihipi Tukairangi, said, "Welcome, O Governor, to Taupo.....I have desired to see Europeans settled at Taupo ever since I first saw them in the Bay of Islands when I signed the Treaty of Waitangi." [16]

It is important to remember that the British were invited to New Zealand by the chiefs. They did not come as military conquerors. During the 1830s the northern chiefs made several approaches to the Government in London for New Zealand to be taken under the wing of the British Crown but Westminster was reluctant until its hand was forced by the New Zealand Company sending out ships crammed with British emigrants.

The most compelling evidence of how the Crown was so welcome in 1840 is the fact that Captain Hobson arrived in a single naval vessel, *HMS Herald*, without troops. Shortly after the signing of the treaty in February, 1840, the *Herald* returned to Sydney, leaving Hobson and his small administrative staff to govern this new territory and virtually at the mercy of the natives.

It was not until 16th April, 1840, that a detachment of 90 British soldiers of the 80th Regiment, under the command of Major Thomas Bunbury, arrived at the Bay of Islands on the naval store ship (not a warship), *HMS Buffalo*, which later sank in Mercury Bay. [17] Thus for two and a half months Hobson and his secretarial staff had no military support and, after these troops arrived, in mid April, they numbered less than a hundred men. That the new sovereign power felt safe enough in this brand new colony and hitherto lawless society is evidence beyond doubt that the Maoris welcomed the arrival of the white man and what he could bring with him.

An obvious conclusion to be drawn from these and numerous other examples of welcome to the white man is that the natives were coming to realise that British settlers would be needed to make a necessary change of character to the country so as to prevent the tribes from falling back into their old ways of warfare and worse.

This was widely recognised. After two decades of British rule and with the settler population now outnumbering the natives, the following chiefs told the Kohimarama Conference of 1860, the largest gathering of chiefs in New Zealand history: Tamihana Te Rauparaha (Ngati Toa): Our tribes are quick in taking up European customs. We are constantly adopting Pakeha customs......The customs of former days have been abandoned....We are now following a new path, and a right one. Let us abandon Maori customs. Look at the superior condition of the Pakeha. This is not slavery".[18]

Wiremu Nero Te Awaitaia (Ngati Mahanga): "We all know what the old customs were, how destructive of human life".[19] Ngati Porou (a message to the conference): "I could not turn back to the evil customs and the cannibalism of our Maori ancestors".[20] Arama Karaka (Te Uriohau, Kaipara): "In the days that are past we were in doubt and uncertainty and knew not whether we should live or die".[21] Kihirini (Tuhourangi, Tarawera): "We have no desire to return to our former way of living".[22] Te Rongotoa: My Maori mother has ceased to exist. You (the Pakeha) shall be my parent for ever and ever".[23]

CONCLUSION

Against all these many and substantial positives of colonisation it is necessary to place any negatives and these appear to be really only two: tobacco and alcohol. It should be pointed out that both of these were and are matters of personal choice and there were numbers of Maoris who partook of neither.

Sometimes the negative effects of smoking were more immediate - as when a native was smoking a pipe while filling cartridges from a 50 pound barrel of gunpowder, pouring the gunpowder into the cartridges with his hand when "a spark fell into the cask, and it is scarcely necessary to say that my poor friend was roasted alive in a second," wrote F.E. Maning. [1] "I have known three other accidents of the same kind, from smoking whilst filling cartridges. In one of these accidents three lives were lost and many injured; and I really believe that the certainty of death will not prevent some of the natives from smoking for more than a given time. I have often seen infants refuse the mother's breast, and cry for the pipe till it was given to them; and dying natives often ask for a pipe, and die smoking." [2]

Tobacco was being grown on the flat-topped Mana Island as early as 1833. "A part of the island [Mana] is already in cultivation and a very fair crop of tobacco was grown there last season," wrote the *Sydney Herald* on 14th August, 1834.

Beer was introduced to New Zealand by Captain Cook on his second voyage in 1773 when he landed at Dusky Sound, near the bottom of the South Island, in the *Resolution*. He brewed some "spruce beer" with leaves and small branches of both a rimu tree and manuka, and molasses (a type of treacle). Most of the crew took to it keenly although probably they had little option since, to promote the new beer, Cook stopped the supply of spirits to the men. The natural historian on board the *Resolution*, Anders Sparrman, liked to mix rum and brown sugar with the ale to make it more palatable. This was New Zealand's first "home brew". Since then alcohol has become a widespread factor in New Zealand life; the solace of many but the curse of some.

******

In 2018 the political commentator, Sir Robert Jones, wrote rather whimsically in one of his columns that New Zealand should have an annual "Maori Gratitude Day" - a day on which part-Maoris could reflect on their good fortune at having been colonised by such a humane, hard working and prosperous people as the British. Oh, the outcry! One loud-mouthed and rather intolerant "film maker", Renae Maihi, screamed that he should be stripped of his knighthood which, of course, didn't and couldn't happen but it did show that this particular "film maker" apparently does not believe in free speech.

The contents of this book, based on written eye-witness accounts of the time, suggest that there would be grounds for such a "Gratitude Day" although it is certainly not what your humble author is advocating.

So, why the hysterical outcry? Because this thing is all about money or, to be more precise, enriching the newly created tribal elite of largely pale skinned people with only one eighth or one sixteenth Maori blood in them - people like Stephen (alias "Tipene") O'Regan, who has made millions of dollars for himself out of the Treaty industry despite being only one sixteenth "Maori". So far more than three billion dollars have been taken from the taxpayer and handed over to various tribes for alleged "historical grievances" for which the Waitangi Tribunal, while rejecting written eye-witness accounts of the time, accepts oral evidence passed down several generations and with an incentive to twist it to suit the case for a claim.

This never-ending multi-billion dollar grievance industry, with the Tribunal dreaming up more and more fictional grounds for raiding the public purse, is based on the huge lie that the colonisation of these anarchic and barbaric islands by the most humane power of the time was so terrible for the native people that their descendants must be forever compensated - even five and six generations down the line when there are no longer any genuine Maoris left - just greedy O'Regans and such similar types who don feathered cloaks and assume Maori names as their part of jumping on a very profitable bandwagon.

And the truly terrible fact - one that has never been reported by the media - is that, although this flow of gold has gone to the leaders of well over a hundred tribes and sub-tribes, not one tribal "leader" has ever been reported as having said "thank-you" to the taxpayer for making these generous and largely undeserved grants. Just a surly "We should have got more". It should be pointed out that this lack of grace, of manners, and of gratitude is displayed by the tribal elite and not by ordinary part-Maoris who must be as appalled as the rest of the country at this greedy - "gimme, gimme, gimme" - attitude.

The contents of this book show beyond all doubt the benefits of colonisation and it is time to put to rest once and for all the lie that colonisation was bad for the Maori. It was, in fact, the most positive and beneficial thing that happened to them in all their history. And much of the credit goes to the Maoris of the time for having the wisdom to accept the new ways, which lifted them out of darkness and insecurity into the light and comfort of modern civilisation.

In the words of Sir Apirana Ngata in his speech at Waitangi during the centenary celebrations of the Treaty in 1940, "That is the outstanding fact to-day; that, but for the seal of the sovereignty handed over to Her Majesty and her descendants, I doubt that there would be a free Maori race in New Zealand to-day."

BIBLIOGRAPHY

One Treaty, One Nation, Hugh Barr et al. Wellington, 2015

The Life of Captain James Cook, J. C. Beaglehole, London, 1974

The Third Wave; Poisoning the Land, W.F. Benfield, Wellington, 2011

The Maori as he was; a brief account of life as it was in Pre-European Days, Elsdon Best. VUW, NZ Electronic Text Collections.

The Albertlanders, Sir Henry Brett and Henry Hook, 1927. Reprinted 2003, Wellsford.

Forty Years in New Zealand, Rev. J. Buller, London, 1878

The First Colonist; Samuel Deighton, 1821-1900, Mike Butler, Wellington, 2010

The Musket Wars, R.D. Crosby, Aucklnad, 2012

Travels in New Zealand, Ernst Dieffenbach, 1843

New Zealand's Changing Biodiversity, Jim Hilton and Roger Childs, Wellington, 2018

The Whalers, Dr. Felix Maynard and Alexandre Dumas, 1937

The Old Whaling Days, Robert McNab, Auckland, 1975

Sweat and Toil; the Building of New Zealand, John McLean, Wellington, 2020

Old New Zealand, F.E. Maning, London, 1863

A Picture Book of Old Hawkes Bay, Kay Mooney and Margaret Henderson, Auckland, 1984

The Treaty of Waitangi; An Explanation, Apirana Ngata, 1922

Narrative of a Voyage to New Zealand, John Liddiard Nicholas, Vols I and II, London, 1818

Cannons Creek to Waitangi, Andy Oakley, Wellington, 2014

Once We Were One, Andy Oakley, Wellington, 2017

The Corruption of New Zealand Democracy,
John Robinson, Wellington, 2011

When Two Cultures Meet; the New Zealand Experience,
John Robinson, Wellington, 2012

Twisting the Treaty, John Robinson et al., Wellington, 2013

Dividing A Nation; the Return to Tikanga,
John Robinson, Wellington, 2019

Unrestrained Slaughter, John Robinson, Wellington, 2020

The Kohimarama Conference, 1860, John Robinson, Wellington, 2022

The Early History of New Zealand, Richard Sherrin and J. H. Wallace.

A History of New Zealand, Keith Sinclair, London, 1980

The Life and Times of Te Rauparaha,
Tamihana Te Rauparaha, VUW, NZ Electronic Text Collection

The Story of New Zealand, A.S. Thomson

The Maori Race, Edward Tregear, New Zealand, 1904. VUW, NZ Electronic Text Collection

Adventure in New Zealand,
Edward Jerningham Wakefield, Wellington, 1908

Te Rou; or the Maori at Home, John White, London, 1874

Christianity Among the New Zealanders,
Rev. William Williams, Edinburgh, 1989

REFERENCES

Chapter 1
A Humanitarian Colonisation
1. P. 356
2. Encyclopedia Britannica, Macropedia, Vol. 18, P. 868
3. Sydney Herald, 22 Nov. 1839
4. P. 10
5. P. 68-9
6. P. 13

Chapter 2
Food
1. Vol. 2, P. 2
2. Nicholas, Vol. 1, P. 190-1
3. White, P. 114
4. The Third Wave; Poisoning the Land, W.F. Benfield, P. 14
5. P. 30
6. The Third Wave; Poisoning the Land, W.F. Benfield, P. 14
7. Vol. 1, P. 315
8. White, P. 48
9. Maning, P. 92-3
10. Nicholas, Vol. 1, P. 84-5
11. Vol. 1, P. 172
12. N.Z. Farmers Weekly, 5 June, 2017
13. Wakefield, P. 113
14. Lyttelton Times, 20 Sept. 1879
15. Waikato Times, 20 March, 1880
16. Thames Advertiser, 20 Feb. 1880
17. Buller, P. 219
18. Diary of John Hemery, 2 March, 1840, MS Papers 4384, Alexander Turnbull Library, Wellington Library, Wellington
19. Maning, P. 57
20. Sydney Herald, 29 July, 1833, Supplement
21. Vol. 2, P. 126-7
22. P. 9
23. The Third Wave; Poisoning the Land, W.F. Benfield, P. 10
24. Wakefield, P. 37

Chapter 3
Clothing
1. Nicholas, Vol. 1, P.130
2. Ibid, P. 131
3. Buller, P. 26
4. Lecture by Dr. Hocken reported in Otago Witness, 18 Sept. 1880
5. Letter from Port Nicholson dated 11 April, 1841. Alexander Turnbull Library MS Papers 3387
6. Diary of *HMS Acheron* reported in Evening Star, Dunedin, 5 June, 1926
7. Christianity Among the New Zealanders, P. 350
8. Maning, P. 210
9. Vol. 1, P. 254

Chapter 4
Housing
1. The Maori As He Was, P. 224
2. Nicholas, Vol. 1, P. 109-110
3. Ibid, P. 96
4. Maning, P. 121
5. P. 16
6. Wakefield, P. 20
7. Nicholas, Vol. 1, P. 175-6
8. P. 112
9. White, P. 310

Chapter 5
Transport
1. Journal of Ten Months Residence in New Zealand, Richard Cruise, entry for 21 Nov. 1820
2. Sweat and Toil, John McLean, P. 238

Chapter 6
Hygiene
1. P.109
2. Nicholas, Vol. 1, P. 87
3. Ibid, P. 282
4. Wakefield, P. 30
5. Ibid, P. 386
6. Nicholas, Vol. 1, P. 301-2
7. Nicholas, Vol. 2, P. 116
8. 12 Sept. 1881
9. Twisting the Treaty, P. 242

Chapter 7
Health
1. White, P. 31
2. Buller, P. 219
3. Nicholas, Vol. 2, P. 130
4. Christianity Among the New Zealanders, P. 184
5. Maning, P. 198
6. Vol. 2, P. 170
7. Ibid
8. Nicholas, Vol. 2, P. 303-4
9. P. 189
10. One Treaty; One Nation, P. 54
11. Nicholas, Vol. 1, P. 88
12. Nicholas, Vol. 2, P. 32

Chapter 8
Superstition
1. P. 19-20
2. P. 198
3. Christianity Among the New Zealanders, William Williams, P. 202-3
4. Wakefield, P. 427-8
5. Wakefield, P. 428
6. One Treaty; One Nation, P. 273
7. P. 273
8. Nicholas, Vol. 2, P. 309-11
9. NZ Herald, 17 August, 1882
10. P. 110
11. Poverty Bay Herald, 1879
12. Otago Daily Times, 9 Nov. 1881
13. Vol 2, P. 112
14. Maning, P. 158-9
15. Nicholas, Vol. 2, P. 30
16. Maori Messenger, 11 July, 1860

Chapter 9
Slavery
1. P. 231
2. P. 312-3
3. Maning, P. 112
4. P. 210-1
5. P. 275
6. P. 178
7. P. 73
8. P. 201
9. White, P. 234
10. P. 181-2
11. P. 224
12. P. 214

Chapter 10
Women
1. History of America, William Robertson, Vol. 2, P. 103
2. Nicholas, Vol. 2, P. 301-2
3. Ibid, P. 312
4. White, P. 63
5. Ibid, P. 57-8
6. Ibid, P. 167-8
7. Ibid, P. 38
8. Nicholas, Vol. 1, P. 177
9. Vol. 2, P. 302-3
10. Christianity Among the New Zealanders, William Williams, P. 156
11. White, P. 153-4
12. Ibid, P. 154-5
13. P. 209
14. Buller, P. 217
15. P. 80
16. Maning, P. 82
17. Diary of *HMS Acheron* as reported in Evening Star, Dunedin, 29 May, 1926
18. Maning, P. 200
19. White, P. 242

Chapter 11
Children
1. Buller, P. 216
2. Ibid, P. 215
3. Ibid, P. 215-6
4. White, P. 54
5. P. 228-9
6. White, P. 237
7. Ibid, P. 224-5
8. Ibid, P. 20
9. Christianity Among the New Zealanders, William Williams, P. 203-4
10. Ibid, P. 4

Chater 12
Infanticide
1. When Two Cultures Meet; the New Zealand Experience, P. 26
2. P. 210
3. Sydney Herald, 3 July, 1837, Sketches of New Zealand
4. J.S. Polack, 1837-8 Parliamentary Papers (British) XXI, 84 as quoted in *New Zealand 1769-1840; Early Years of Western Contact*, H.M. Wright, Harvard Historical Monographs, 42, P.57
5. P. 68
6. Sydney Herald, 20 March, 1837

Chapter 13
Tribal Warfare
1. Otago Witness, 18 Sept. 1880
2. P. 244
3. P. 23
4. Captain Cook's Voyages, 1768-1779, G. Williams, editor, Folio Society, London, 1997, P. 76
5. P. 249
6. Unrestrained Slaughter, John Robinson, P. 88
7. Christianity Among the New Zealanders, William Williams, P. 74
8. Unrestrained Slaughter, John Robinson, P. 87
9. Christianity Among the New Zealanders, William Williams, P. 235
10. The Corruption of New Zealand Democracy, John Robinson, P. 18
11. Diary of *HMS Acheron* as reported in Evening Star, Dunedin, 22 May, 1926
12. Wikipedia - "Musket Wars"
13. P. 73
14. Ibid
15. P. 79
16. Unrestrained Slaughter, John Robinson, P. 112-3
17. The Penguin History of New Zealand, Michael King, 2003, P. 134
18. Unrestrained Slaughter, John Robinson, P. 113
19. Rutherford paper undated, as quoted in When Two Cultures Meet; the New Zealand Experience, John Robinson, P. 43
20. P. 17
21. University of Minnesota, College of Liberal Arts, Holocaust and Genocide Studies - Cambodia)
22. Wikipedia
23. P. 5
24. Maning, P. 185
25. P. 64

Chapter 14
Cannibalism
1. Nicholas, Vol. 2, P. 62
2. Unrestrained Slaughter, John Robinson, P. 82
3. The Musket Wars, R.D. Crosby, P. 228
4. Unrestrained Slaughter, John Robinson, P. 82, and Dr. Hocken lecture reported in Otago Witness, 18 Sept. 1880
5. Vol 2, P. 63
6. Ibid, P. 68
7. Ibid, P. 69
8. Buller, P. 250
9. Nicholas, Vol. 2, P. 218-9
10. Christianity Among the New Zealanders, William Williams, P. 240
11. The Whalers, Felix Maynard and Alexandre Dumas, P. 324
12. White, P. 233

13. as quoted in The Early History of New Zealand, Richard Sherrin and J.H. Wallace, P.183
14. The Old Whaling Days, Robert McNab, P. 56-7
15. Ibid, P. 45
16. as quoted in The Early History of New Zealand, Richard Sherrin and J.H. Wallace, P.181
17. Ibid
18. Sydney Herald, 25 Jan. 1836
19. P. 235
20. The Early History of New Zealand, Richard Sherrin and J.H. Wallace, P. 182
21. The Old Whaling Days, R. McNab, Appendix C, P. 424
22. P. 183
23. as quoted in Christianity Among the New Zealanders, William Williams, P. 26-7

Chapter 15
Property Rights
1. Twisting the Treaty, P. 52
2. Ibid, P. 52-3
3. Vol. 1, P. 277-8
4. P. 78
5. P. 54
6. Twisting the Treaty, P. 54-5
7. Christianity Among the New Zealanders, William Williams, P. 299
8. Ibid, P. 311-2
9. Ibid, P. 349-50
10. Nicholas, Vol. 1, P.238
11. Twisting the Treaty, P. 58
12. Reply from Ngapuhi, 14 July, 1860, as quoted in The Kohimarama Conference 1860, John Robinson, P. 85
13. P. 93
14. Buller, P. 487
15. The Treaty of Waitangi; An Explanation, A. Ngata, P. 37
16. AJHR 1928 G 07,
    Page 11 - paragraph 15;
    Page 17 - paragraph 35;
    Page 19 - paragraph 42;
    Page 21 - paragraph 56
17. NZ Herald, 31 Jan. 1881

Chapter 16
Introduction of Law
1. The Life of Captain James Cook, J.C. Beaglehole, P. 359
2. Vol. 2, P. 309
3. A show of justice, racial amalgamation in nineteenth century New Zealand, A.Ward, 1973, P. 32;
   Taua, A. Ballara, 2003, P.429-31;
   The Years Before Waitangi; a story of Early Maori/European Contact in New Zealand, P.M. Bawden, 1987, P.144-5;
   Two Great New Zealanders, John Robinson, P.69-71
4. Buller, P. 490
5. P. 92-3
6. Maning, P. 80
7. Capt. Hobson to H.E. Lt. Gen. Sir Richard Bourke, Governor of NSW, Enclosure A,Visit of *HMS Rattlesnake* to New Zealand, 1837, as quoted in Once We Were One, Andy Oakley, P. 142

8. P. 143
9. P. 35
10. Shortland, Auckland Standard, 9 May, 1842
11. Maori Messenger Reports on Kohimarama Conference, 2 August, 1860
12. Ibid, 23 July, 1860
13. The Kohimarama Conference 1860, John Robinson, P. 82
14. Maori Messenger Reports on Kohimarama Conference, 11 and 18 July, 1860
15. The Treaty of Waitangi; An Explanation, A. Ngata
16. Wakefield, P. 198-9
17. Maning, P. 68
18. Dividing A Nation; the Return to Tikanga, John Robinson, P. 160
19. Unrestrained Slaughter, John Robinson, P. 74-5
20. P. 13
21. NZCPR, 9 May, 2021
22. Stuff News, 14 October, 2021
23. When Two Cultures Meet; the New Zealand Experience, John Robinson, P. 20
24. The Treaty of Waitangi, An Explanation, A. Ngata

Chapter 17
Language
1. Good Reasons for Reading, Stephen Pimenoff, Daily Telegraph, London. Undated
2. Southern Cross, 12 June, 1872
3. Ibid
4. P. 105

Chapter 18
Fauna and Flora
1. P. 33
2. New Zealand's Changing Biodiversity, Jim Hilton and Roger Childs, P. 31
3. Ibid, P. 25, and Envirohistory NZ website
4. P. 13 and 17
5. Chambers Journal, Edinburgh, No. 257, Vol. 9, 1848
6. NZ Gazette, 5 Dec. 1840
7. P. 40-1
8. New Zealand's Changing Biodiversity, Jim Hilton and Roger Childs, P. 42-3
9. Wakefield, P. 485
10. Southern Cross, 17 September, 1862
11. The Third Wave; Poisoning the Land, W.F. Benfield, P. 25
12. P. 27 and 30

Chapter 19
Population
1. P. 13-14
2. P. 187-92
3. The Corruption of New Zealand Democracy, John Robinson, P. 90
4. P. 85
5. When Two Cultures Meet; the New Zealand Experience, John Robinson, P. 62

Chapter 20
Welcome, White Man
1. Vol. 1
2. P.16
3. P.364
4. P.24
5. Wakefield, P.52
6. Ibid, P. 56
7. Ibid, P. 52
8. J.H. Wallace, as quoted in The First Colonist, Mike Butler, Wellington, 2010. P.21
9. Wakefield, P.97-8
10. NZ Heritage, Vol. 2, P. 423
11. A Picture Book of Old Hawkes Bay, Kay Mooney and Margaret Henderson, P. 10
12. NZ Herald, 4 Nov. 1892, P.11
13. West Coast Times, 22 Dec. 1873, P.2
14. The Albertlanders, Sir Henry Brett and Henry Hook, P.239
15. The Pioneering McLeods of Helensville, John McLean, 2012, P.27
16. Southern Cross, 12 June, 1872
17. Evening Post, Wellington, 22 Oct. 1920, P.8
18. Maori Messenger reports on the Kohimarama Conference 1860. 17 July, 1860
19. Ibid, 1 August, 1860
20. Ibid, 16 July, 1860
21. Ibid, 3 August, 1860
22. Ibid, 18 July, 1860
23. Ibid, 12 July, 1860

Chapter 21
Conclusion
1. P.35
2. Maning, P.3

INDEX

A
HMS Acheron 19-20, 29, 53
HMS Alligator 77
Anscow, Mr. 45-6
Ardern, Jacinda 63

B
Benfield, W.F. 16, 98, 102
Best, Elsdon 22, 24, 30, 33
Bourke, Governor 88
Bowen, Sir George 97, 113
Brash, Don 38
Buck, Sir Peter 66, 68
HMS Buffalo 114
Buller, Rev. J. 18, 43, 47, 52, 60, 64, 65, 72, 83, 87, 109
Bunbury, Major Thomas 114

C
Carroll, Sir James 31
Childs, Roger 98, 101
Churchman, Peter 91-2, 93, 94
Clark, Helen 89
Cook, Captain 10, 11, 12, 16, 19, 65, 71, 86, 109, 115
Cresswell, Peter 79, 80
Crosby R.D. 67
Cruise, Richard 27

D
Davis, Rev. 57
Deighton, Richard and Samuel 110
Dieffenbach, Ernst 40

HMS Dromedary 13, 26, 27
Duaterra, Chief 34, 82
Dumas, Alexandre 76

E
Earle, Mr. 75

F
Faraday, Michael 25
Finlayson, Christopher 71

G
Gittos, Rev. W. 112
Glazebrook, Susan 89, 91, 93, 94
Guard, John 77
Gutenberg, Johannes 96

H
Hansard, Mr. 53
Hape, Hiria 92
Hau, Wiremu 86
Hauraki, Doug 92
Hemery, Captain John 15
HMS Herald 114
Heuheu, Chief 37
Hilton, Jim 98, 101
Himiona 88
Hobson, Capt. 88, 100, 114
Hocken, Dr. 64
Hongi Hika 66, 96

J
Jones, Sir Robert 116

K
Karaitiana, Chief 41
Kempton, Thomas 19
Kendall, Thomas 35, 96
Khan, M.A. 42
King, Michael 67

L
Lee, Prof. Samuel 96
Lyon, Mr. 100

M
Macdonnell, Lieut. 13
Mackintosh, Charles 20
McLean, John 38-9
McLeod, John 113
Maihi, Renae 116
Maning, F.E. 16, 20, 34, 35, 37, 40, 53, 88, 89, 106, 109, 115
Marsden, Rev. Samuel 9, 12, 13, 20, 30, 31, 34, 40, 82, 86
Maynard, Felix 76
Maze, Joanna 38
Midland Railway Co. 28
Moon, Bruce 109

N
Ngata, Sir Apirana 31, 84, 89, 94, 117
Nicholas, John 9, 11, 12, 16, 20, 22, 24, 30, 31, 34, 35, 48, 51, 70, 71, 72, 80, 82, 86, 109
Nobel, Alfred 28

O
Oakley, Andy 69, 88
O'Regan, Stephen (alias Tipene) 116
Orman, Tony 101
Oxley, Catherine 113

P
HMS Pandora 29
Petre, Lord 102
Pihana 39
Polack, Joel 45, 60
Pomare, Maui 31
Powell, Grant 93, 94
Puakawa, Chief 15

R
HMS Rattlesnake 88
Rawton, John and William 77
HMS Resolution 115
Robinson, John 7, 8, 31, 60, 64, 66, 88, 90, 93, 94, 103, 107
Rontgen, Wilhelm 36
Rutherford, Prof. James 67

S
Shacklock, Henry 11
Sheridan, Daniel 73, 75
Sherrin, Richard 45, 78
Shortland, Edward 100
Sinclair, Prof. Keith 7, 80
Singer, Isaac 20
Smith, Stephenson Percy 67
Smith, William 77
Sparrman, Anders 115
Stewart, Capt. 70
Stokes, Robert 112

T
Tapsell, Mr. 66
Tawhiao, Chief 39
Te Kume, Reweti 97
Te Maiharanui 7126, 43, 66, 71, 110
Te Puni 109-10, 111
Te Rangihaeata 43
Te Rauparaha 26, 43, 66, 71, 110
Te Rauparaha, Tamihana 20, 88
Te Whero, Wiremu 88
Te Whero Whero 88
Te Whiti 14, 18, 25, 39-40
Thomson, A.S. 73
Tohikura, Hapurona 88
Tohu 39
Touai 73
Tukairangi, Poihipi 97, 113
Turner, Nathaniel 61

W
Wahanui, Chief 39
Waharoa, Chief 73
Waikato, Chief 96
Waitangi Tribunal 71, 90
Waititi, Rawiri 36
Wakefield, Edward Jerningham 13, 17, 23, 30, 37, 43, 68, 89, 109, 111
Wallace, John H. 45, 78, 110
West, James 77
Wharepouri 109-110
White, James 77
White, John 10, 23, 42, 44, 46, 51, 54, 55
White, William 28
Williams, Joe 89-91, 93, 94
Williams, Rev. William 5, 20, 33, 37, 44, 51, 58, 67, 81-2
Willis, Mrs. 102
Willy, Anthony 92
Wilson, Ormond 61

Y
Yate, Rev. William 19